SCIENTIFIC AMERICAN EXPLORES BIG IDEAS

Understanding Consciousness

The Editors of *Scientific American*

SCIENTIFIC AMERICAN EDUCATIONAL PUBLISHING

New York

Published in 2024 by Scientific American Educational Publishing
in association with **The Rosen Publishing Group**
2544 Clinton Street, Buffalo NY 14224

Contains material from Scientific American®, a division of Springer Nature America, Inc., reprinted by permission, as well as original material from The Rosen Publishing Group®.

First Edition

Scientific American
Lisa Pallatroni: Project Editor

Rosen Publishing
Erica Grove: Compiling Editor
Michael Moy: Senior Graphic Designer

Cataloging-in-Publication Data

Names: Scientific American, Inc.
Title: Understanding consciousness / edited by the Scientific American Editors.
Description: First Edition. | New York : Scientific American Educational Publishing, 2024. | Series: Scientific American explores big ideas | Includes bibliographic references and index.
Identifiers: ISBN 9781725349698 (pbk.) | ISBN 9781725349704 (library bound)| ISBN 9781725349711 (ebook)
Subjects: LCSH: Consciousness. | Consciousness–Miscellanea. | Parapsychology.
Classification: LCC B105.C477 U534 2024 | DDC 128'.2–dc23

Manufactured in the United States of America
Websites listed were live at the time of publication.

Cover: Lidiia/Shutterstock.com

CPSIA Compliance Information: Batch # SACS24.
For Further Information contact Rosen Publishing at 1-800-237-9932.

CONTENTS

INTRODUCTION

To many, consciousness is a defining aspect of human experience. It is how you feel, what you think, what you perceive, what you like, and how you see yourself and the world around you. The inner life of the conscious mind is one of the fundamental mysteries that have enthralled the medical, psychological, and philosophical communities for years. It is a mystery that—if solved—would exponentially increase our understanding of ourselves and the existential dilemmas we commonly experience.

The idea of consciousness has fascinated humankind and been a source of philosophical and scientific debate since the French philosopher René Descartes first introduced the concept of mind–body dualism in the 16th century—and possibly even earlier, with some claiming the Greek philosopher Aristotle was the first to theorize on consciousness in the 300s BCE (though he did not use the term "consciousness"). According to Descartes' mind–body dualism, the essential nature of the mind is different from that of the rest of the body, and consciousness resides in the mind, not the physical matter of the body (which includes the brain).

However, despite Descartes' claim that consciousness cannot be located in physical matter such as the brain, since the late 19th century—but becoming particularly popular starting in the mid-20th century—scientists have been researching the brain to try to understand the scientific basis of consciousness. Neurologists have attempted to locate the neural underpinnings of consciousness out of certainty that there has to be a material, biological explanation for how we experience it. But so far, developing a definitive theory of where consciousness is located in the brain has proven elusive, though many scientists now believe that the cerebral cortex is mostly responsible for consciousness.

In recent decades, questions of consciousness have expanded to include non-human forms as well. Some scientists have begun to study animal consciousness, attempting to determine if animals exhibit conscious behaviors like emotion, pain and suffering, and self-consciousness, and the extent to which animal consciousness may be similar to that experienced by humans. The dramatic expansion of the artificial intelligence (AI) has also raised questions of whether machines can in some way also be conscious.

This volume explores a wide range of perspectives covering these questions and more. In Section 1, "The Mind, the Brain, and Consciousness," we consider articles on what consciousness is and neuroscientific research exploring where it may be located in the brain. Section 2—"Altered States of Consciousness"—examines how drugs, brain injuries, anesthesia, and mental illness can affect consciousness and how this can help us better understand consciousness. In Section 3, "Is Consciousness Uniquely Human?," explores the question of whether animals, machines, and other matter can be considered conscious. Finally, Section 4—"Can Consciousness Be Explained by Science?"—considers viewpoints on what scientific research can and cannot clarify about consciousness.

Section 1: The Mind, the Brain, and Consciousness

What Is Consciousness?

By Christof Koch

Consciousness is everything you experience. It is the tune stuck in your head, the sweetness of chocolate mousse, the throbbing pain of a toothache, the fierce love for your child and the bitter knowledge that eventually all feelings will end.

The origin and nature of these experiences, sometimes referred to as qualia, have been a mystery from the earliest days of antiquity right up to the present. Many modern analytic philosophers of mind, most prominently perhaps Daniel Dennett of Tufts University, find the existence of consciousness such an intolerable affront to what they believe should be a meaningless universe of matter and the void that they declare it to be an illusion. That is, they either deny that qualia exist or argue that they can never be meaningfully studied by science.

If that assertion was true, this essay would be very short. All I would need to explain is why you, I and most everybody else is so convinced that we have feelings at all. If I have a tooth abscess, however, a sophisticated argument to persuade me that my pain is delusional will not lessen its torment one iota. As I have very little sympathy for this desperate solution to the mind-body problem, I shall move on.

The majority of scholars accept consciousness as a given and seek to understand its relationship to the objective world described by science. More than a quarter of a century ago Francis Crick and I decided to set aside philosophical discussions on consciousness (which have engaged scholars since at least the time of Aristotle) and instead search for its physical footprints. What is it about a highly excitable piece of brain matter that gives rise to consciousness? Once we can understand that, we hope to get closer to solving the more fundamental problem.

We seek, in particular, the neuronal correlates of consciousness (NCC), defined as the minimal neuronal mechanisms jointly sufficient for any specific conscious experience. What must happen in your brain for you to experience a toothache, for example? Must some nerve cells vibrate at some magical frequency? Do some special "consciousness neurons" have to be activated? In which brain regions would these cells be located?

Neuronal Correlates of Consciousness

When defining the NCC, the qualifier "minimal" is important. The brain as a whole can be considered an NCC, after all: it generates experience, day in and day out. But the seat of consciousness can be further ring-fenced. Take the spinal cord, a foot-and-a-half-long flexible tube of nervous tissue inside the backbone with about a billion nerve cells. If the spinal cord is completely severed by trauma to the neck region, victims are paralyzed in legs, arms and torso, unable to control their bowel and bladder, and without bodily sensations. Yet these tetraplegics continue to experience life in all its variety–they see, hear, smell, feel emotions and remember as much as before the incident that radically changed their life.

Or consider the cerebellum, the "little brain" underneath the back of the brain. One of the most ancient brain circuits in evolutionary terms, it is involved in motor control, posture and gait and in the fluid execution of complex sequences of motor movements. Playing the piano, typing, ice dancing or climbing a rock wall–all these activities involve the cerebellum. It has the brain's most glorious neurons, called Purkinje cells, which possess tendrils that spread like a sea fan coral and harbor complex electrical dynamics. It also has by far the most neurons, about 69 billion (most of which are the star-shaped cerebellar granule cells), four times more than in the rest of the brain combined.

What happens to consciousness if parts of the cerebellum are lost to a stroke or to the surgeon's knife? Very little! Cerebellar patients complain of several deficits, such as the loss of fluidity of piano playing or keyboard typing but never of losing any aspect of their consciousness. They hear, see and feel fine, retain a sense of self, recall past events and continue to project themselves into the future. Even being born without a cerebellum does not appreciably affect the conscious experience of the individual.

All of the vast cerebellar apparatus is irrelevant to subjective experience. Why? Important hints can be found within its circuitry, which is exceedingly uniform and parallel (just as batteries may be connected in parallel). The cerebellum is almost exclusively a feed-forward circuit: one set of neurons feeds the next, which in turn influences a third set. There are no complex feedback loops that reverberate with electrical activity passing back and forth. (Given the time needed for a conscious perception to develop, most theoreticians infer that it must involve feedback loops within the brain's cavernous circuitry.) Moreover, the cerebellum is functionally divided into hundreds or more independent computational modules. Each one operates in parallel, with distinct, nonoverlapping inputs and output, controlling movements of different motor or cognitive systems. They scarcely interact—another feature held indispensable for consciousness.

One important lesson from the spinal cord and the cerebellum is that the genie of consciousness does not just appear when any neural tissue is excited. More is needed. This additional factor is found in the gray matter making up the celebrated cerebral cortex, the outer surface of the brain. It is a laminated sheet of intricately interconnected nervous tissue, the size and width of a 14-inch pizza. Two of these sheets, highly folded, along with their hundreds of millions of wires—the white matter—are crammed into the skull. All available evidence implicates neocortical tissue in generating feelings.

We can narrow down the seat of consciousness even further. Take, for example, experiments in which different stimuli are presented to the right and the left eyes. Suppose a picture of Donald Trump is visible only to your left eye and one of Hillary Clinton only to your right eye. We might imagine that you would see some weird superposition of Trump and Clinton. In reality, you will see Trump for a few seconds, after which he will disappear and Clinton will appear, after which she will go away and Trump will reappear. The two images will alternate in a never-ending dance because of what neuroscientists call binocular rivalry. Because your brain is getting an ambiguous input, it cannot decide: Is it Trump, or is it Clinton?

If, at the same time, you are lying inside a magnetic scanner that registers brain activity, experimenters will find that a broad set of cortical regions, collectively known as the posterior hot zone, is active. These are the parietal, occipital and temporal regions in the posterior part of cortex that play the most significant role in tracking what we see. Curiously, the primary visual cortex that receives and passes on the information streaming up from the eyes does not signal what the subject sees. A similar hierarchy of labor appears to be true of sound and touch: primary auditory and primary somatosensory cortices do not directly contribute to the content of auditory or somatosensory experience. Instead it is the next stages of processing–in the posterior hot zone–that give rise to conscious perception, including the image of Trump or Clinton.

More illuminating are two clinical sources of causal evidence: electrical stimulation of cortical tissue and the study of patients following the loss of specific regions caused by injury or disease. Before removing a brain tumor or the locus of a patient's epileptic seizures, for example, neurosurgeons map the functions of nearby cortical tissue by directly stimulating it with electrodes. Stimulating the posterior hot zone can trigger a diversity of distinct sensations and feelings. These could be flashes of light, geometric shapes, distortions of faces, auditory or visual hallucinations, a feeling of familiarity or unreality, the urge to move a specific limb, and so on. Stimulating the front of the cortex is a different matter: by and large, it elicits no direct experience.

A second source of insights are neurological patients from the first half of the 20th century. Surgeons sometimes had to excise a large belt of prefrontal cortex to remove tumors or to ameliorate epileptic seizures. What is remarkable is how unremarkable these patients appeared. The loss of a portion of the frontal lobe did have certain deleterious effects: the patients developed a lack of inhibition of inappropriate emotions or actions, motor deficits, or uncontrollable repetition of specific action or words. Following the operation, however, their personality and IQ improved, and they went on to live for many more years, with no evidence that the drastic removal of frontal tissue significantly affected their conscious experience. Conversely, removal of even small regions of the posterior cortex, where the hot zone resides, can lead to a loss of entire classes of conscious content: patients are unable to recognize faces or to see motion, color or space.

So it appears that the sights, sounds and other sensations of life as we experience it are generated by regions within the posterior cortex. As far as we can tell, almost all conscious experiences have their origin there. What is the crucial difference between these posterior regions and much of the prefrontal cortex, which does not directly contribute to subjective content? The truth is that we do not know. Even so—and excitingly—a recent finding indicates that neuroscientists may be getting closer.

The Consciousness Meter

An unmet clinical need exists for a device that reliably detects the presence or absence of consciousness in impaired or incapacitated individuals. During surgery, for example, patients are anesthetized to keep them immobile and their blood pressure stable and to eliminate pain and traumatic memories. Unfortunately, this goal is not always met: every year hundreds of patients have some awareness under anesthesia.

Another category of patients, who have severe brain injury because of accidents, infections or extreme intoxication, may live for years without being able to speak or respond to verbal requests. Establishing that they experience life is a grave challenge to the clinical arts. Think of an astronaut adrift in space, listening to mission control's attempts to contact him. His damaged radio does not relay his voice, and he appears lost to the world. This is the forlorn situation of patients whose damaged brain will not let them communicate to the world—an extreme form of solitary confinement.

In the early 2000s Giulio Tononi of the University of Wisconsin–Madison and Marcello Massimini, now at the University of Milan in Italy, pioneered a technique, called zap and zip, to probe whether someone is conscious or not. The scientists held a sheathed coil of wire against the scalp and "zapped" it—sent an intense pulse of magnetic energy into the skull—inducing a brief electric current in the neurons underneath. The perturbation, in turn, excited and inhibited the neurons' partner cells in connected regions, in a chain reverberating across the cortex, until the activity died out. A network of electroencephalogram (EEG) sensors, positioned outside the skull, recorded these electrical signals. As they unfolded over time, these traces, each corresponding to a specific location in the brain below the skull, yielded a movie.

These unfolding records neither sketched a stereotypical pattern, nor were they completely random. Remarkably, the more predictable these waxing and waning rhythms were, the more likely the brain was unconscious. The researchers quantified this intuition by compressing the data in the movie with an algorithm commonly used to "zip" computer files. The zipping yielded an estimate of the complexity of the brain's response. Volunteers who were awake turned out have a "perturbational complexity index" of between 0.31 and 0.70, dropping to below 0.31 when deeply asleep or anesthetized. Massimini and Tononi tested this zap-and-zip measure on 48 patients who were brain-injured but responsive and awake, finding that in every case, the method confirmed the behavioral evidence for consciousness.

The team then applied zap and zip to 81 patients who were minimally conscious or in a vegetative state. For the former group, which showed some signs of nonreflexive behavior, the method correctly found 36 out of 38 patients to be conscious. It misdiagnosed two patients as unconscious. Of the 43 vegetative-state patients in which all bedside attempts to establish communication failed, 34 were labeled as unconscious, but nine were not. Their brains responded similarly to those of conscious controls—implying that they were conscious yet unable to communicate with their loved ones.

Ongoing studies seek to standardize and improve zap and zip for neurological patients and to extend it to psychiatric and pediatric patients. Sooner or later scientists will discover the specific set of neural mechanisms that give rise to any one experience. Although these findings will have important clinical implications and may give succor to families and friends, they will not answer some fundamental questions: Why these neurons and not those? Why this particular frequency and not that? Indeed, the abiding mystery is how and why any highly organized piece of active matter gives rise to conscious sensation. After all, the brain is like any other organ, subject to the same physical laws as the heart or the liver. What makes it different? What is it about the biophysics of a chunk of highly excitable brain matter that turns gray goo into the glorious surround sound and Technicolor that is the fabric of everyday experience?

Ultimately what we need is a satisfying scientific theory of consciousness that predicts under which conditions any particular physical system—whether it is a complex circuit of neurons or silicon transistors—has experiences. Furthermore, why does the quality of these experiences differ? Why does a clear blue sky feel so different from the screech of a badly tuned violin? Do these differences in sensation have a function, and if so, what is it? Such a theory will allow us to infer which systems will experience anything. Absent a theory with testable predictions, any speculation about machine consciousness is based solely on our intuition, which the history of science has shown is not a reliable guide.

Fierce debates have arisen around the two most popular theories of consciousness. One is the global neuronal workspace (GNW) by psychologist Bernard J. Baars and neuroscientists Stanislas Dehaene and Jean-Pierre Changeux. The theory begins with the observation that when you are conscious of something, many different parts of your brain have access to that information. If, on the other hand, you act unconsciously, that information is localized to the specific sensory motor system involved. For example, when you type fast, you do so automatically. Asked how you do it, you would not know: you have little conscious access to that information, which also happens to be localized to the brain circuits linking your eyes to rapid finger movements.

Toward a Fundamental Theory

GNW argues that consciousness arises from a particular type of information processing—familiar from the early days of artificial intelligence, when specialized programs would access a small, shared repository of information. Whatever data were written onto this "blackboard" became available to a host of subsidiary processes: working memory, language, the planning module, and so on. According to GNW, consciousness emerges when incoming sensory information, inscribed onto such a blackboard, is broadcast globally to multiple cognitive systems—which process these data to speak, store or call up a memory or execute an action.

Because the blackboard has limited space, we can only be aware of a little information at any given instant. The network of neurons that broadcast these messages is hypothesized to be located in the frontal and parietal lobes. Once these sparse data are broadcast on this network and are globally available, the information becomes conscious. That is, the subject becomes aware of it. Whereas current machines do not yet rise to this level of cognitive sophistication, this is only a question of time. GNW posits that computers of the future will be conscious.

Integrated information theory (IIT), developed by Tononi and his collaborators, including me, has a very different starting point: experience itself. Each experience has certain essential properties. It is intrinsic, existing only for the subject as its "owner"; it is structured (a yellow cab braking while a brown dog crosses the street); and it is specific—distinct from any other conscious experience, such as a particular frame in a movie. Furthermore, it is unified and definite. When you sit on a park bench on a warm, sunny day, watching children play, the different parts of the experience—the breeze playing in your hair or the joy of hearing your toddler laugh—cannot be separated into parts without the experience ceasing to be what it is.

Tononi postulates that any complex and interconnected mechanism whose structure encodes a set of cause-and-effect relationships will have these properties—and so will have some level of consciousness. It will feel like something from the inside. But if, like the cerebellum, the mechanism lacks integration and complexity, it will not be aware of anything. As IIT states it, consciousness is intrinsic causal power associated with complex mechanisms such as the human brain.

IIT theory also derives, from the complexity of the underlying interconnected structure, a single nonnegative number Φ (pronounced "*fy*") that quantifies this consciousness. If Φ is zero, the system does not feel like anything to be itself. Conversely, the bigger this number, the more intrinsic causal power the system possesses and the more conscious it is. The brain, which has enormous and highly specific connectivity, possesses very high Φ, which implies a high level of consciousness. IIT explains a number of observations, such as why the cerebellum does not contribute to consciousness and why the zap-and-zip meter works. (The quantity the meter measures is a very crude approximation of Φ.)

IIT also predicts that a sophisticated simulation of a human brain running on a digital computer cannot be conscious—even if it can speak in a manner indistinguishable from a human being. Just as simulating the massive gravitational attraction of a black hole does not actually deform spacetime around the computer implementing the astrophysical code, programming for consciousness will never create a conscious computer. Consciousness cannot be computed: it must be built into the structure of the system.

Two challenges lie ahead. One is to use the increasingly refined tools at our disposal to observe and probe the vast coalitions of highly heterogeneous neurons making up the brain to further delineate the neuronal footprints of consciousness. This effort will take decades, given the byzantine complexity of the central nervous system. The other is to verify or falsify the two, currently dominant, theories. Or, perhaps, to construct a better theory out of fragments of these two that will satisfactorily explain the central puzzle of our existence: how a three-pound organ with the consistency of tofu exudes the feeling of life.

This article is part of a special report, "The Biggest Questions in Science," sponsored by The Kavli Prize. It was produced independently by Scientific American *and* Nature *editors, who have sole responsibility for all the editorial content.*

About the Author

Christof Koch is chief scientist of MindScope at the Allen Institute for Brain Science and of the Tiny Blue Dot Foundation, as well as author of The Feeling of Life Itself—Why Consciousness Is Widespread but Can't Be Computed *(MIT Press, 2019). He is on Scientific American's board of advisers.*

Self-Awareness with a Simple Brain

By Ferris Jabr

The computer, smartphone or other electronic device on which you may be reading this article, tracking the weather or checking your e-mail has a kind of rudimentary brain. It has highly organized electrical circuits that store information and behave in specific, predictable ways, just like the interconnected cells in your brain. On the most fundamental level, electrical circuits and neurons are made of the same stuff—atoms and their constituent elementary particles—but whereas the human brain is conscious of itself, man-made gadgets do not *know* they exist.

Consciousness, most scientists would argue, is not a shared property of all matter in the universe. Rather consciousness is restricted to a subset of animals with relatively complex brains. The more scientists study animal behavior and brain anatomy, however, the more universal consciousness seems to be. A brain as complex as a human's is definitely not necessary for consciousness. On July 7 of this year, a group of neuroscientists convening at the University of Cambridge signed a document entitled "The Cambridge Declaration on Consciousness in Non-Human Animals," officially declaring that nonhuman animals, "including all mammals and birds, and many other creatures, including octopuses," are conscious.

Humans are more than just conscious; they are also self-aware. Scientists differ on how they distinguish between consciousness and self-awareness, but here is one common distinction: consciousness is awareness of your body and your environment; self-awareness is recognition of that consciousness—not only understanding that you exist but further comprehending that you are aware of your existence. Another way of considering it: to be conscious is to think; to be self-aware is to realize that you are a thinking being and to think about your thoughts. Presumably human infants are conscious—they perceive and respond to people and things around them—but they are not yet self-aware. In their first years of life, children develop a sense of self, learning to recognize themselves in the mirror and to distinguish between their own point of view and the perspectives of other people.

Numerous neuroimaging studies have suggested that thinking about ourselves, recognizing images of ourselves, and reflecting on our thoughts and feelings—that is, different forms of self-awareness—all involve the cerebral cortex, the outermost, intricately wrinkled part of the brain. The fact that humans have a particularly large and wrinkly cerebral cortex relative to body size supposedly explains why we seem to be more self-aware than most other animals. But new evidence is casting doubt on this idea.

"Got a Towel?"

If this anatomical hypothesis were correct, we would expect, for example, that a man missing huge portions of his cerebral cortex would lose at least some of his self-awareness. Patient R, also known as Roger, defies that expectation. Roger is a 57-year-old man who suffered extensive brain damage in 1980 after a severe bout of herpes simplex encephalitis, an inflammation of the brain caused by herpesvirus. The disease destroyed most of Roger's insular cortex, anterior cingulate cortex and medial prefrontal cortex, regions near or at the front surface of the brain that are thought to be essential for self-awareness. About 10 percent of his insula remains and only 1 percent of his anterior cingulate cortex.

Roger cannot remember much of what happened to him between 1970 and 1980, and he has great difficulty forming new memories. He cannot taste or smell either. But he still knows who he is. He recognizes himself in the mirror and in photographs, and his behavior is relatively normal.

In a paper published earlier this year postdoctoral researcher Carissa L. Philippi of the University of Wisconsin–Madison and neuroscientist David Rudrauf of the University of Iowa and their colleagues investigated the extent of Roger's self-awareness. In a mirror-recognition task, for example, a researcher pretended to brush something off of Roger's nose with a tissue that concealed black eye shadow. Fifteen minutes later the researcher asked Roger to look at himself in the mirror. Roger immediately rubbed away the black smudge on his nose and wondered aloud how it got there.

The researchers also showed Roger pictures of himself, of people he knew and of strangers. He almost always recognized himself and never mistook another person for himself. He did sometimes have difficulty recognizing a photo of his face when it appeared by itself on a black background, without any hair or clothing.

Roger also distinguished the sensation of tickling himself from the feeling of someone else tickling him and consistently found the latter more stimulating. When one researcher asked for permission to tickle Roger's armpits, he replied, "Got a towel?" As Philippi and Rudrauf note, Roger's quick wit indicates that in addition to maintaining a sense of self, he adopts the perspective of others—a talent known as theory of mind. He anticipated that the researcher would notice his sweaty armpits and used humor to preempt any awkwardness.

In another task, Roger had to use a computer mouse to drag a blue box from the center of a computer screen toward a green box in one of the corners of the screen. In some cases, the program gave him complete control over the blue box; in other cases, the program restricted his control. Roger easily discriminated between sessions in which he had full control and times when some other force was at work. In other words, he understood when he was and was not responsible for certain actions.

Given the evidence of Roger's largely intact self-awareness, Philippi, Rudrauf and their colleagues argue that the insular cortex, anterior cingulate cortex and medial prefrontal cortex cannot by themselves account for conscious recognition of oneself as a thinking being. Instead they propose that self-awareness is a far more diffuse cognitive process, relying on many parts of the brain, including regions not located in the cerebral cortex.

Laughing without a Brain

In the new study, Philippi, Rudrauf and their co-authors point to a fascinating 1999 review of children with hydranencephaly, a rare disorder in which fluid-filled sacs replace the brain's cerebral hemispheres. Children with hydranencephaly are essentially missing every part of their brain except for the brain stem and cerebellum and a few other structures. Holding a light near such a child's head illuminates the skull like a jack-o'-lantern.

Although many children with hydranencephaly appear relatively normal at birth, they often quickly develop growth problems, seizures and impaired vision. Most die within a year; some live for years or even decades. Such children lack a cerebral cortex, but at least a few give every appearance of genuine consciousness. They respond to people and things in their environment. They smile, laugh and cry. They know the difference between familiar people and strangers. And they prefer some kinds of music to others. If some children with hydranencephaly are conscious, then the brain does not require an intact cerebral cortex to produce consciousness.

Whether such children are truly self-aware is more difficult to answer, especially as they cannot communicate with language. In the 1999 review one child showed intense fascination with his reflection in a mirror, but it is not clear whether he recognized his reflection as his own. Still, research on hydranencephaly and Roger's case study indicate that self-awareness–this ostensibly sophisticated and unique cognitive process layered on consciousness–might be more universal than we realized.

Referenced

Consciousness in Congenitally Decorticate Children: Developmental Vegetative State as Self-Fulfilling Prophecy. D. A. Shewmon, G. L. Holmes and P. A. Byrne in *Developmental Medicine and Child Neurology*, Vol. 41, No. 6, pages 364–374; June 1999.

Consciousness without a Cerebral Cortex: A Challenge for Neuroscience and Medicine. B. Merker in *Behavioral and Brain Sciences*, Vol. 30, pages 63–81; 2007.

Preserved Self-Awareness following Extensive Bilateral Brain Damage to the Insula, Anterior Cingulate, and Medial Prefrontal Cortices. Carissa L. Philippi et al. in *PLoS ONE*, Vol. 7, No. 8; August 2012.

About the Author

Ferris Jabr is an associate editor at Scientific American. *He is our guest columnist, filling in for Christof Koch, who writes Consciousness Redux.*

Is Consciousness Real?

By John Horgan

Of all the odd notions to emerge from debates over consciousness, the oddest is that it doesn't exist, at least not in the way we think it does. It is an illusion, like "Santa Claus" or "American democracy."

Descartes said consciousness is the one undeniable fact of our existence, and I find it hard to disagree. I'm conscious right now, as I type this sentence, and you are presumably conscious as you read it. (I can't be sure about you, because I have access only to my own consciousness.)

The idea that consciousness isn't real has always struck me as crazy, and not in a good way, but smart people espouse it. One of the smartest is philosopher Daniel Dennett, who has been questioning consciousness for decades, notably in his 1991 bestseller *Consciousness Explained*.

I've always thought I must be missing something in Dennett's argument, so I hoped his new book, *From Bacteria to Bach and Back: The Evolution of Minds*, would enlighten me. It does, but not in the way Dennett intended.

Dennett restates his claim that Darwinian theory can account for all aspects of our existence. We don't need an intelligent designer, or "skyhook," to explain how eyes, hands and minds came to be, because evolution provides "cranes" for constructing all biological phenomena.

Natural selection yields what Dennett calls "competence without comprehension." (D.D. loves alliteration.) Even the simplest bacterium is a marvelous machine, extracting from its environment what it needs to survive and reproduce. Eventually, the mindless, aimless process of evolution produced *Homo sapiens*, a species capable of competence *and* comprehension.

But human cognition, Dennett emphasizes, *still* consists mainly of competence without comprehension. Our conscious thoughts represent a minute fraction of all the information processing carried out by our brains. Natural selection designed our brains to provide us with thoughts on a "need to know" basis, so we're not overwhelmed with data.

Dennett compares consciousness to the user interface of a computer. The contents of our awareness, he asserts, bear the same relation to our brains that the little folders and other icons on the screen of a computer bear to its underlying circuitry and software. Our perceptions, memories and emotions are grossly simplified, cartoonish representations of hidden, hideously complex computations.

None of this is novel or controversial. Dennett is just reiterating, in his oh-so-clever, neologorrheic fashion, what mind-scientists and most educated lay folk have long accepted, that the bulk of cognition happens beneath the surface of awareness. Dennett even thanks the much-vilified Sigmund Freud for his "championing of unconscious motivations"!

Trouble arises when Dennett, extending the computer-interface analogy, calls consciousness a "user-*illusion*." I italicize *illusion*, because so much confusion flows from Dennett's use of that term. An illusion is a false perception. Our thoughts are *imperfect* representations of our brain/minds and of the world, but that doesn't make them necessarily false.

Take this thought: "Donald Trump is a narcissistic jerk." That is an extremely compressed statement about an extremely messy external reality. Moreover, my ability to think the thought, or type it on my laptop, depends on complex hardware and software, the workings of which I am happily ignorant. But that doesn't mean "Donald Trump is a narcissistic jerk" is an *illusion*, any more than "2 + 2 = 4."

What if I think "2 + 2 = 5," "Global warming is a hoax" or "Donald Trump is the wisest man on earth"? What if I am psychotic, or living in a simulation created by evil robots, and *all* my thoughts are illusions? To say my consciousness is therefore an illusion would be to conflate *consciousness* with its contents. That's like saying a book doesn't exist if it depicts non-existent things. And yet that is what Dennett seems to suggest.

Consider how Dennett talks about qualia, philosophers' term for subjective experiences. My *qualia* at this moment are the smell of coffee, the sound of a truck rumbling by on the street, my puzzlement over Dennett's ideas. Dennett notes that we often overrate the objective accuracy and causal power of our qualia. True enough.

But he concludes, bizarrely, that therefore qualia are fictions, "an artifact of bad theorizing." If we lack qualia, then we are zombies, creatures that look and even behave like humans but have no inner, subjective life. Imagining a reader who insists he is not a zombie, Dennett writes:

"The only support for that conviction [that you are not a zombie] is the vehemence of the conviction itself, and as soon as you allow the theoretical possibility that there *could* be zombies, you have to give up your papal authority about your own nonzombiehood." Think you're conscious? Think again.

Dennett gets annoyed when critics accuse him of saying "consciousness doesn't exist," and to be fair, he never flatly makes that claim. His point seems to be, rather, that consciousness is so insignificant, especially compared to our exalted notions of it, that it *might as well* not exist.

Dennett's arguments are so convoluted that he allows himself plausible deniability, but he seems to be advocating eliminative materialism, which the *Stanford Encyclopedia of Philosophy* defines as "the radical claim that our ordinary, common-sense understanding of the mind is deeply wrong and that some or all of the mental states posited by common-sense do not actually exist."

Other philosophers call consciousness "the hard problem" because of the yawning "explanatory gap" between physiological processes and subjective, mental states. Eliminative materialists say there is no hard problem or explanatory gap because there are no subjective phenomena, or at least none worth worrying about.

When I encounter a baffling belief, at some point I stop trying to understand it and focus on the believer. What's the motive?

Why would Dennett expend so much energy advancing such a preposterous position?

Like many philosophers, Dennett clearly gets a kick out of defending positions that defy common sense. But his primary agenda is defending science against religion and other irrational belief systems. Dennett, an outspoken atheist, fears that creationism and other superstitious nonsense will persist as long as mysteries do. He thus insists that science can untangle even the knottiest conundrums, including the origin of life (which he asserts that recent "breakthroughs" are helping to solve) and consciousness.

Dennett accuses those who question science's power of bad faith. These doubters don't want their "beloved mysteries" explained. Dennett can't accept that anyone might have legitimate, rational reasons for resisting his reductionist vision.

One prominent doubter is philosopher Thomas Nagel, who in "What Is It Like to be a Bat?" and other writings explores why consciousness is unlikely to yield to conventional scientific analysis. Reviewing *From Bacteria to Bach*, Nagel rebukes Dennett thus:

> "To say that there is more to reality than physics can account for is not a piece of mysticism: it is an acknowledgement that we are nowhere near a theory of everything, and that science will have to expand to accommodate facts of a kind fundamentally different from those that physics is designed to explain."

Some people surely have an unhealthy attachment to mysteries, but Dennett has an unhealthy aversion to them, which compels him to stake out unsound positions. His belief that consciousness is an illusion is nuttier than the belief that God is real. Science has real enemies—some in positions of great power–but Dennett doesn't do science any favors by shilling for it so aggressively.

Let me nonetheless conclude by thanking Dennett. Agree with him or not, I always find him provocative and entertaining. And by forcing me to pay closer attention to my awareness, his eliminative outlook has roused me from my normal torpor. This zombie can always use a little more consciousness.

The views expressed are those of the author(s) and are not necessarily those of Scientific American.

About the Author

John Horgan directs the Center for Science Writings at the Stevens Institute of Technology. His books include The End of Science, The End of War and Mind-Body Problems, *available for free at mindbodyproblems.com. For many years he wrote the popular blog Cross Check for* Scientific American.

Think of Consciousness as Art Created by the Brain

By Nicholas Humphrey

Consciousness matters to us. Many would say it matters more than anything. We relish the beauty of a winter sunset, the memory-fueled comforts of a homecoming, the inviting caress of a lover's hand. Conscious sensations lie at the core of our being. Without access to this marvel, we'd be poorer creatures living in a duller world. Yet the fundamental nature of consciousness remains a scientific mystery. The problem is not that we do not understand consciousness at all—some aspects of it are relatively easy to explain. The problem is that one aspect of it continues to baffle everyone, and that's the "feel" or "phenomenal character" of consciousness—or, as philosopher Thomas Nagel has put it, simply "what it is like." Biologist H. Allen Orr probably speaks for most scientists when, in a recent review of Nagel's book *Mind and Cosmos*, he writes: "I ... share Nagel's sense of mystery here. Brains and neurons obviously have everything to do with consciousness, but how such mere objects can give rise to the eerily different phenomenon of subjective experience seems utterly incomprehensible."

Theorists tend to fall into one of two camps. Some assert that the manifestly eerie and ineffable qualities of subjective experience can only mean that these nonphysical qualities are inherent in the fabric of the universe. Others, including me, are more suspicious. They argue that consciousness may be more like a conjuring show, whereby the physical brain is tricking people into believing in qualities that don't really exist.

But no one wants to be told the latter story! So I am going to try telling the story in a different way. While I believe consciousness may indeed be a stage trick by the brain, I want to suggest that it is also a stroke of artistic genius. Consciousness as art is surely a more palatable notion than consciousness as illusion. I am not just looking to make friends for a theory that may be hard to swallow; I also want to influence the further questions scientists ask.

The Experience of Pain

Suppose you prick your thumb. Your brain responds to signals from the thumb with an internalized hurt response, the neural correlate of pain. From an objective point of view, this response is nothing more than the activity of nerve cells. From your subjective point of view, however, this experience seems to be nothing less than—well—conscious pain.

Yet how can this transformation possibly occur? How can there be physical matter on one side of the equation and nonphysical consciousness on the other? Philosophers talk about the existence of an "explanatory gap" here. As Colin McGinn has put it, "You might as well assert that numbers emerge from biscuits or ethics from rhubarb."

I am a scientist. But when the philosophical skeptics put it like that, I agree they may be right. You really can't get numbers from biscuits, and you really can't get pain from nerve cells, at any rate not if the pain is conceived of as some kind of alchemical substance exuded by the brain.

But what if this is simply the wrong way to conceive of pain? What if pain is nothing other than your "inner picture" of the neural activity? And what if this picture is actually pure make-believe—part of your brain's internal conjuring show?

These are some big what-ifs, and we should tread carefully. I may be convinced that some such explanation must be true, but other theorists treat the idea with incredulity and even scorn. In her book *Are You an Illusion?* British philosopher Mary Midgley's answer is to pinch herself, feel the reality of the sensation and say, in effect, "Don't be daft."

Midgley balks at the suggestion that she is an illusion because she takes it to imply she is some kind of mistake. But let's try telling the story in another way. How about suggesting that when you see red or taste a lemon, your brain is creating something like a cubist painting—not necessarily a misrepresentation but an artistic *re*-presentation of the facts? Would Midgley feel better if she could be persuaded that she is actually a remarkable work of art?

Consciousness, Defined

Let's step back so we can place this new idea in the context of consciousness in general. The "eerily different phenomenon" to which Orr drew attention may still prove to be the sticking point. But we should not assume at the start that everything about consciousness is impossibly difficult. Indeed, the first steps toward a scientific understanding are straightforward and have already been taken.

We should begin with a definition. Although opinions differ, I think it is helpful to start by describing consciousness simply as introspective access to mental states. That is to say, you, the subject of consciousness, are conscious of mental states—perceptions, memories, wishes, and so on—just insofar as you know about them by looking in on your own mind.

Note that we encounter only one you here. When you feel pain, or you want breakfast, or you remember your mother's face, it's the same you in each case. This unity is not a logical necessity. It is theoretically possible your brain could have housed several independent versions of you, each representing a different module of the mind. Indeed, you may actually have started out this way at birth. As your life got going and your body began interacting with the world, however, the separate subjects soon became orchestrated as one. Your perceiving self, your remembering self, your acting self became merged into the one big you.

The unity of the self underlies the most obvious function of consciousness: namely to provide a mind-wide forum for planning and decision making. Your brain has brought information from different modules to the same table, as it were, to allow fertile cross talk. This integration opens the way for a central processing unit to recognize patterns, marry past and future, assign priorities, and so on. Computer programmers might call this central processor an "expert system," rather like an intelligent autopilot. You call the onboard pilot "I."

With all this activity happening on a single stage, consciousness has become something like a theater, where the engine of the mind is on show. You find you can reflect on what's going on. And this capacity for self-reflection supports a second important function of consciousness: to allow you to appreciate how your mind works. Observing, for example, how beliefs and desires generate wishes that lead to actions, you find your mind revealed as having a clear psychological structure. You begin to gain insight into why you think and act the way you do: you can explain yourself to yourself and explain yourself to other people, too. What's more, you have a model for explaining other people to yourself. Consciousness has laid the ground for what psychologists call "theory of mind."

So far so good. We have a definition, two important functions for consciousness and a suggestive metaphor, the theater of consciousness. We have not yet had to raise the question of illusion, and—for that reason perhaps—nothing about this account of consciousness seems completely incomprehensible. In fact, neuroscientists are already making considerable headway in discovering how the brain could realize some of these features. Stanislas Dehaene of the Collège de France in Paris has been mapping what he calls "the global neuronal workspace." Giulio Tononi of the University of Wisconsin–Madison has proposed a statistical model of "integrated information." Christof Koch of the Allen Institute for Brain Science in Seattle (who serves on *Scientific American*'s board of advisers) has identified a brain structure, the claustrum, as a likely candidate for the master of ceremonies.

The Eerie Quality

Hold on, however. The picture that is emerging may not be incomprehensible but neither is it eerie. Where's the peculiar what-it-is-like-ness that Nagel pointed to? Where's the phenomenal quality philosophers beef about?

We should note that the quality in question does not pervade every aspect of consciousness. In fact (although not everyone agrees), I'd say this quality is not a feature of higher levels of cognition. There is no "what it is like" for you to have the thought that two plus two is four. Rather this quality seems to kick in only at a more animal level, in the way you represent what's happening at your bodily sense organs. Of the variety of mental states of which you're conscious, it is your sensations—and only your sensations—that have this peculiar dimension to them.

The special qualities of sensations are what philosophers call "qualia." Although scientists don't often use that term, there's no denying that qualia present natural science with a spectacular challenge. Koch wrote to me not long ago that "it is bizarre that brain matter should exude these phenomenal feelings. Consciousness is so vivid, and its properties appear so otherworldly, that it seems to call for God." He may have been half-joking. But who's laughing? Short of invoking some supernatural agency, where are we to go?

Most theorists now accept that only two options can be taken seriously, along the dividing line I sketched earlier. We can be realists about qualia, or else we have to be illusionists. Unfortunately, both options come at a considerable price.

Eeriness of consciousness changes your sense of who and what you are. It feeds your self-worth, your joy in life, your fear of death. Perhaps the evolutionary function of "consciousness as art" is to make you fall in love with the artist—yourself.

Realists take qualia at face value. In their view, if your sensations appear to have qualities that lie beyond the scope of physics, then they really do have such qualities. And these realists explain their reasoning by suggesting that the brain activity underlying sensations already has consciousness latent in it as an additional property of matter—a property as yet unrecognized by physics but one that you, the conscious subject, are somehow able to tap into. The price for this explanation is that it implies that the standard physical description of the world is radically incomplete.

Illusionists take the contrary line. If your sensations appear to have these qualities, then your physical brain is playing tricks on you. Your brain can pull off such magical effects because it houses a computational engine that deals in symbols, and physically based symbols can perfectly well represent states of affairs that do not and could not exist. The price for this explanation is that it devalues not only the mystery but the majesty of the core experience.

Art Rather than Illusion

I belong, as I said, to the illusionist camp, and I've provided extensive psychological and evolutionary arguments for my position over the years. But even if illusionism is scientifically correct, I well understand why it is not the story many people want to hear. So now let me try sweetening the pill. Why might it be more persuasive if we were to talk about qualia as art rather than illusion? I am not proposing an alternative theory to illusionism, but my hope is that shifting the emphasis in a positive direction may in fact make the illusionist theory more scientifically acute and at the same time more humanly agreeable.

First, we generally consider illusions to be sources of error, but we think of works of art as sources of enlightenment. In Pablo Picasso's words, "Art is a lie that makes us realize truth." Or in Paul Klee's, "Art does not reproduce the visible; rather it makes visible." Or in Friedrich Nietzsche's, "Art is not merely imitation of the reality of nature but rather a metaphysical supplement to the reality of nature." Ellen Dissanayake, a writer on art and evolution, has characterized art in general as the activity of "making special." By likening sensations to works of art, therefore, we can emphasize how ordinary information from the sense organs is transformed and embellished on the way to consciousness.

Next, we tend to think of illusions as fortuitous or accidental, but we think of works of art as necessarily involving an artist. So now we can draw attention to the active agency behind conscious sensations. The immediate agent–if not the ultimate designer–is your own brain, when it responds to sensory information by creating the neural correlates of qualia. Neuroscientists do not yet know what these neural correlates amount to (although I have made some detailed suggestions in my book *Soul Dust*). Could it be your brain employs some of the same aesthetic principles that artists use?

Furthermore, as Marcel Duchamp said, "The artist performs only one part of the creative process. The onlooker completes it, and it is the onlooker who has the last word." Art necessarily implicates an audience. So now we can also draw attention to your self as the reactive and appreciative observer of the brain art. Moreover, drawing on what we know about art appreciation, we can go on to ask how you evaluate qualia, cognitively and emotionally. Are there individual differences in susceptibility to the illusory message? Do people learn to read qualia, as they learn to appreciate art? What does it take to become a qualia connoisseur?

Last and most important, we seldom regard illusions as having any human value, but we expect works of art to be intellectually and spiritually nourishing, good for our souls. We don't care to be dupes of an illusion, but we are proud to be art lovers. Thus, this way of thinking about sensations allows us to look out for–and celebrate–the psychological growth that human beings derive from participating in the self-made show.

The Beauty of Consciousness

The chief scientific bonus of conceptualizing consciousness as art may prove to be precisely this: that it raises new questions for an evolutionist about the value and purpose of consciousness. If sensations are art, the artist behind them is actually not the individual brain as such. Rather the artist–the ultimate designer–must be the evolutionary forces of natural selection, which have contrived to put in place the genetic code for building the qualia-generating brain. Yet natural selection promotes only variants that contribute to biological survival. What then can be the biological advantage of a brain that delivers such awe-inspiring but seemingly superfluous flummery?

The analogy with art continues to help. Charles Darwin struggled to explain several of the more exotic features of animal courtship until he hit on the idea that such displays are designed not to serve any obvious utilitarian purpose but rather to show off—and to seduce. The peacock's gaudy tail does not enable him to fly any higher, but it raises his status in the eyes of the peahen. Darwin suggested that one of the chief functions of human art, too, is to induce the onlooker to fall in love with the artist.

Thus, an extraordinary possibility suggests itself: the evolutionary function of brain art is nothing less than to induce you to fall in love with yourself. The qualia of visual sensation, for example, are not necessary to your perception of the outside world, but—along with all your other sensations—they enlarge your sense of who you are. Qualia feed your self-worth, your joy in life, your fear of death. Nor is this idle speculation. In my book *Seeing Red*, I describe a remarkable case of a woman with a form of "blindsight"—vision without conscious qualia—whose sense of self seemed to be so damaged that she became suicidal.

French philosopher René Descartes famously intoned: "I think, therefore I am." But the self that evolves around sensory consciousness is deeper and more generous: I feel, therefore I am. Therefore you feel, and you are, too. Consciousness, by placing you at the center of this brilliant and perplexing work of art, encourages you to think of all humans as equally touched by magic. Thus, you end up, though by a different route, just where Midgley, Nagel and others want you to be: as centers of spiritual excellence, spreading the joy.

Referenced

Soul Dust: The Magic of Consciousness. Nicholas Humphrey. Princeton University Press, 2011.

Consciousness and the Brain. Stanislas Dehaene. Viking, 2014.

A Riddle Written on the Brain. Nicholas Humphrey in *Journal of Consciousness Studies*, Vol. 23, Nos. 7–8, pages 278–287; May 2016.

The Footprints of Consciousness. Christof Koch in *Scientific American Mind*, Vol. 28, No. 2, pages 52–59; March/April 2017.

The Magic of Consciousness. Royal Institution video, with Nicholas Humphrey: www.youtube.com/watch?v=NHXCi6yZ-eA

About the Author

Nicholas Humphrey is emeritus professor of psychology at the London School of Economics and a professor at Darwin College, Cambridge. He won the 2015 Mind & Brain Prize.

Constant Shifts between Mental States Mark a Signature of Consciousness

By Simon Makin

Imagine driving to work along the same route you take each day. Your mind wanders from one thing to the next: the staff meeting in the afternoon, plans for the weekend, a gift you need to buy for a friend. Suddenly, a car cuts you off, and these thoughts immediately vanish—all of your attention focuses on maneuvering the steering wheel to avoid a collision. Although momentarily flustered, you—and your thoughts—return to the same wandering pattern a minute or two later.

As we go about our waking lives, our stream of consciousness typically cycles through many such alternations between introspection and outward attention throughout the day. It appears that the back-and-forth dance between these inward and outward mental states may be fundamental to brain function. A new study, led by neuroscientist Zirui Huang of the Center for Consciousness Science at the University of Michigan, suggests that the shifting balance between a network responsible for awareness of the environment and another responsible for awareness of self may be a defining feature of consciousness.

The evidence comes from the absence of this pattern of brain activity in people rendered unresponsive, whether by anesthesia or a neuropathologic condition. As well as advancing our understanding of consciousness, the work could lead to the development of techniques to monitor it, either prior to surgery or during the treatment of people with disorders of consciousness, such as vegetative or "locked-in" patients.

Over the past two decades, neuroscientists have identified a network of brain regions responsible for various kinds of introspection, from mind wandering to recollection and planning. The concept of "background" brain activity began drawing attention when neurologist Marcus Raichle and his colleagues at Washington University in St. Louis showed that the organ's energy consumption rose by less than 5 percent when performing a focused mental task, suggesting it is never really idle. In 2001 Raichle coined the term "default mode" to describe this activity. Converging lines of evidence then led to identification of regions comprising the default mode network (DMN), which underlies this self-directed cognition.

Activity in the DMN is "anticorrelated" with activity in the so-called dorsal attention network (DAT): the more active one of the two networks is, the less active the other tends to be. Activity in the DAT corresponds to attention directed outward, while the DMN underlies consciousness of self. This arrangement provides a potential account of our conscious experience in terms of a reciprocal balance between two opposing neural networks. "It's not an either-or thing; you're just tipping a balance," Raichle says. "We slide back and forth, but they're both there to some degree."

A portion of this research has remained controversial because of a method used to clean noise from brain scan data that some researchers argue will always generate anticorrelated patterns as an artifact of processing the data. In the study, published Wednesday in *Science Advances*, Huang and his colleagues avoided the issue by adopting an approach that did not use this processing method. They instead took advantage of machine-learning techniques to classify brain activation patterns into eight groups. Two of them corresponded to the DMN and DAT, and six are related to other known networks underlying brain functions: the sensory and motor network, the visual network, the ventral attention network, the frontoparietal network and two networks representing cross-brain states of activation and deactivation.

To capture the brain activity, the team used a technique called resting-state functional magnetic resonance imaging (rsfMRI). Rather than averaging activity over long periods, which is typically done when using rsfMRI to estimate how well-connected regions are, the researchers wanted to investigate how moment-to-moment brain activation unfolds over time.

They showed that the organ rapidly cycles through different states, corresponding to each of the eight networks, with some transitions being more probable than others–which Huang describes as a "temporal circuit. " Notably, the brain passes through intermediate states between DMN and DAT activation rather than flipping instantaneously between these two extremes, which represents the highest-level cognitive processes.

The researchers scanned 98 participants, who were either lying still but conscious or in an unresponsive state. The latter was caused by propofol or ketamine anesthesia or by a neuropathological condition known as unresponsive wakefulness syndrome–a vegetative condition resulting from brain injury. All of these unresponsive states had one thing in common: the DMN and DAT were "isolated" from the constant flitting between networks of the temporal circuit, and they virtually never activated.

Each type of unresponsiveness varied in terms of the molecular mechanisms, neural circuits and experiences involved (those under ketamine anesthesia reported hallucinations, for instance). These observations could indicate that the absence of DMN-DAT activity is common to any form of diminished consciousness and that its presence may be a necessary feature of full consciousness. "What [the researchers are] suggesting here is: if you mess with that balance, you see a cost in consciousness," says Raichle, who was not involved in the study. "It's an interesting way to frame [DMN-DAT activity], and it's descriptive of our consciousness. But does it explain it? I'm not sure."

In another experiment, the researchers showed that playing a sound increased activation of the ventral attention network (which redirects our attention to unexpected stimuli) and suppressed activation of the DMN in conscious participants but not in unresponsive ones. A final control experiment assessed network activation in a database of brain scans of psychiatric patients. The scientists found no difference between this group and conscious participants in terms of DMN and DAT activity, showing that its loss is specific to reduced responsiveness, not any form of disordered cognition.

There also were differences among the various unresponsive states. For instance, participants given ketamine more frequently entered cross-brains states of activation and deactivation. This pattern was also seen in schizophrenic patients' scans, suggesting hyperactivated patterns may correspond to hallucinatory experiences common to both ketamine use and schizophrenia. "If all the processors share information everywhere in the brain, I guess you may lose the difference between yourself and the environment," Huang says. "Everything occurs at once, and you have distortions of your mental content."

The work could potentially be used to develop measures of consciousness for assessing the efficacy of treatments for disorders of consciousness or for online monitoring of anesthesia. "Once we see the two networks are diminished, we think individuals aren't aware of their environment," Huang says. Measures to gauge whether an individual is conscious or not could assist physicians in the surgical suite. He next plans to investigate the neural mechanisms that regulate these transitions in the temporal circuit comprising these brain networks—an exploration of what orchestrates the dancing dynamics of conscious activity.

About the Author

Simon Makin is a freelance science journalist based in the U.K. His work has appeared in New Scientist, *the* Economist, Scientific American *and* Nature, *among others. He covers the life sciences and specializes in neuroscience, psychology and mental health. Follow Makin on Twitter @SimonMakin.*

Section 2: Altered States of Consciousness

Transcending the Brain

By Bernardo Kastrup

Despite significant advances in neuroscience, consciousness remains a vexing mystery. Because the qualities of experience seem to be irreducible to physical parameters,[1] a hypothesis that has been garnering attention is that consciousness is fundamental and spatially unbound, the brain corresponding to a dissociation or localization of its contents.[2] At first sight, simple observation seems to contradict this hypothesis: as pointed out by neuroscientist Sam Harris, if a normally functioning brain corresponds to a limitation of cognition,

> ...one would expect most forms of brain damage to unmask extraordinary scientific, artistic, and spiritual insights.... A few hammer blows or a well-placed bullet should render a person of even the shallowest intellect a spiritual genius. Is this the world we are living in?

Harris's rhetorical question alludes to the indisputable fact that most forms of brain function impairment correlate with cognitive deficit. However, a more interesting question is perhaps this: Do *some* forms of impairment correlate with an enrichment of consciousness or cognitive skill? After all, even if only one black swan can be conclusively discerned in a herd of white swans, our theories about the origin and nature of swans must be able to make sense of those black individuals.

As it turns out, there are reliable reports in the medical literature of—yes—bullet wounds to the head, stroke, concussion, meningitis, and even the progression of dementia leading to expanded cognitive and artistic skills.[3] Ironically, therefore, Harris' rhetorical question has an affirmative answer: somehow, this is indeed the world we are living in.

And that's just the tip of the iceberg. Many forms of brain function impairment associated with seeming unconsciousness are now known to be accompanied by richer inner life. For instance, the dangerous "choking game" played by teenagers worldwide[4] is an attempt to induce rich feelings of self-transcendence through partial strangulation and fainting.[5] The psychotherapeutic technique of holotropic breathwork[6] also uses hyperventilation-induced fainting to achieve what is described as an expansion of awareness.[7] Even pilots undergoing "G-force induced Loss Of Consciousness" (G-LOC)—whereby blood is forced out of the brain—report "memorable dreams."[8]

Generalized physiological stress caused, for instance, by cardiac arrest—which severely compromises brain function—is sometimes accompanied by reports of "Near Death Experiences" (NDEs).[9] NDEs reportedly entail life-transforming insights, emotions and inner imagery far richer than ordinary experiences,[10] despite overwhelming disruption to the brain's ability to operate.

This pattern of correlations between brain function impairment and a seeming expansion of awareness is surprisingly broad. For instance, during the practice of so-called "psychography," an alleged medium enters a trance state and writes down information allegedly originating from a transcendent source. A detailed neuroimaging study revealed that experienced mediums displayed marked reduction of activity in key brain regions—such as the frontal lobes and hippocampus—when compared to regular, non-trance writing.[11] Despite this, text written under trance scored consistently higher in a measure of complexity than material produced without trance.

Even more intriguingly, it is well known that psychedelic substances induce powerful experiences of self-transcendence.[12] It had been assumed that they did so by *exciting* parts of the brain. Yet, recent neuroimaging studies have shown that psychedelics do largely the opposite.[13] Moreover, "the magnitude of this decrease [in brain activity] predicted the intensity of the subjective effects."[14] In other words, the less activated the brain becomes, the more intense the psychedelic experiences.

If this pattern is consistent, we should expect some types of physical brain damage to also lead to experiences of self-transcendence. And indeed, this has been reported. In a recent study, CT scans of more than one hundred Vietnam war veterans showed that damage to the frontal and parietal lobes increased the likelihood of "mystical experiences."[15] In an earlier study, patients were evaluated before and after brain surgery for the removal of tumors, which caused collateral damage to surrounding tissue. Statistically significant increases in "feelings of self-transcendence" were reported after the surgery.[16]

Clearly, there is a broad and consistent pattern associating impairment of brain function with–in the words of Harris–"extraordinary scientific, artistic, and spiritual insights." That this happens in but a small minority of cases isn't surprising: damage affecting memory pathways, metacognition, language centers, or any other cognitive function necessary for recalling or reporting inner life erases the signs of such insights. A person lying in a vegetative state could be having indescribably rich inner experiences and we would be none the wiser. The evidence is necessarily constrained to a narrow window between brain function impairment insufficient to trigger self-transcendence and impairment that renders self-transcendence unreportable to self or others.

It is conceivable that brain function impairment could disproportionally affect inhibitory neural processes, thereby generating or bringing into awareness other neural processes associated with self-transcendence. However, if experience is constituted, generated, or at least fully modulated by brain activity, an increase in the richness of experience must be accompanied by an increase in the metabolism associated with the neural correlates of experience.[17] Any other alternative would decouple experience from the workings of the living brain information-wise. As such, it is difficult to see how partial strangulation, hyperventilation, G-LOC, cardiac arrest, etc.–which reduce oxygen supply to the brain as a whole–could selectively affect inhibitory neural processes whilst preserving enough oxygen supply to fuel an increase in the neural correlates of experience.

Alternatively, one could speculate that experiences of self-transcendence occur only *after* normal brain function resumes. This, however, cannot account for several of the cases mentioned. For instance, during the neuroimaging studies of the psychedelic state researchers collected subjective reports of self-transcendence while *concurrently* monitoring the subjects' *reduced* brain activity levels. The same holds for the neuroimaging study of psychography. Finally, in cases of acquired savant syndrome the savant skills are often *concomitant* with the presence of physical damage in the brain.

It is conceivable that individual cases of self-transcendence could have their own idiosyncratic explanation, unrelated to the other cases, and that the overall pattern suggested here is a red herring. However, all cases mentioned here, besides being associated with brain function impairment, also share strikingly consistent subjective reports. Consider the two passages below:

> *Passage 1:*
>
> I certainly don't feel reduced or smaller in any way. On the contrary, I haven't ever been this huge, this powerful, or this all-encompassing. ... [I] felt greater and more intense and expansive than my physical being.[18]
>
> *Passage 2:*
>
> My perception of my physical boundaries was no longer limited to where my skin met air. I felt like a genie liberated from its bottle. The energy of my spirit seemed to flow like a great whale gliding through a sea of silent euphoria.[19]

Passage 1 was reported by the subject of an NDE caused by generalized physiological stress, while passage 2 was reported by the subject of a stroke.

Such similarities suggest that normal brain function corresponds to a dissociation or localization of the contents of consciousness, and that certain forms of impairment of brain function reduce this dissociation or localization, thereby leading to expanded awareness and self-transcendence. The implications of this hypothesis for both neuroscience and neurophilosophy are far-reaching.

This essay is based on the paper "Self-Transcendence Correlates with Brain Function Impairment," published in the Journal of Cognition and Neuroethics, *volume 4, number 3, pp. 33-42.*

Notes

1. Chalmers (2003).
2. Kastrup (2015), pp. 10-36, Shani (2015), and Nagasawa and Wager (Forthcoming).
3. Lythgoe et al. (2005), Treffert (2006), Treffert (2009), p. 1354, Piore (2013), Miller et al. (1998), and Miller et al. (2000).
4. Macnab (2009).
5. Neal (2008), 310-315.
6. Rhinewine & Williams (2007).
7. Taylor (1994).

8 Whinnery & Whinnery (1990).

9. van Lommel (2001).
10. Kelly et al. (2009), 367-421.
11. Peres (2012).
12. Strassman (2001), Griffiths et al. (2006), and Strassman et al. (2008).

13 Carhart-Harris et al. (2012), Palhano-Fontes et al. (2015), and Carhart-Harris et al. (2016).

14. Carhart-Harris et al. (2012), 2138.
15. Cristofori (2016).
16. Urgesi et al. (2010).
17. Kastrup (2016).
18. Moorjani (2012), 69.
19. Taylor (2009), 67.

Referenced

Carhart-Harris, R. L. et al. 2012. "Neural correlates of the psychedelic state as determined by fMRI studies with psilocybin." *Proceeding of the National Academy of Sciences of the United States of America* 109 (6): 2138-2143.

Carhart-Harris, R. L. et al. 2016. "Neural correlates of the LSD experience revealed by multimodal neuroimaging." *Proceeding of the National Academy of Sciences of the United States of America (PNAS Early Edition),* doi: 10.1073/pnas.1518377113.

Chalmers, D. 2003. "Consciousness and its place in nature." In: S. Stich & F. Warfield (eds.). *Blackwell Guide to the Philosophy of Mind*. Malden, MA: Blackwell.

Cristofori, I. et al. 2016. "Neural correlates of mystical experience." *Neuropsychologia* 80: 212-220.

Griffiths, R. R. et al. 2006. "Psilocybin can occasion mystical-type experiences having substantial and sustained personal meaning and spiritual significance." *Psychopharmacology* 187: 268-283.

Kastrup, B. 2015. *Brief Peeks Beyond: Critical essays on metaphysics, neuroscience, free will, skepticism and culture*. Winchester, UK: Iff Books.

Kastrup, B. 2016. "What Neuroimaging of the Psychedelic State Tells Us about the Mind-Body Problem." *Journal of Cognition and Neuroethics* 4 (2): 1-9.

Kelly, E. F. et al. 2009. *Irreducible Mind: Toward a Psychology for the 21st Century*. Lanham, MD: Rowman & Littlefield.

Lythgoe, M. et al. 2005. "Obsessive, prolific artistic output following subarachnoid hemorrhage." *Neurology* 64: 397-398.

Macnab, A. J. et al. 2009. "Asphyxial games or 'the choking game': a potentially fatal risk behavior." *Injury Prevention* 14: 45-49.

Miller, B. et al. 1998. "Emergence of artistic talent in frontotemporal dementia." *Neurology* 51: 978-982.

Miller, B. et al. 2000. "Functional correlates of musical and visual ability in frontotemporal dementia." *The British Journal of Psychiatry* 176: 458-463.

Moorjani, A. 2012. *Dying to Be Me: My Journey from Cancer, to Near Death, to True Healing*. Carlsbad, CA: Hay House.

Nagasawa, Y. and Wager, K. Forthcoming. "Panpsychism and Priority Cosmopsychism." In: Brüntrup, G. and Jaskolla, L. (eds.). *Panpsychism*. Oxford, UK: Oxford University Press.

Neal, R. M. 2008. *The Path to Addiction: And Other Troubles We Are Born to Know*. Bloomington, IN: AuthorHouse.

Palhano-Fontes, F. et al. 2015. "The Psychedelic State Induced by Ayahuasca Modulates the Activity and Connectivity of the Default Mode Network." *PLoS ONE* 10 (2): e0118143.

Peres, J. et al. 2012. "Neuroimaging during Trance State: A Contribution to the Study of Dissociation." *PLoS ONE* 7 (11): e49360.

Piore, A. 2013. "The Genius Within." *Popular Science March*: 46-53.

Rhinewine, J. P. and Williams, O. J. 2007. "Holotropic Breathwork: The Potential Role of a Prolonged, Voluntary Hyperventilation Procedure as an Adjunct to Psychotherapy." *The Journal of Alternative and Complementary Medicine* 13 (7): 771-776.

Shani, I. 2015. "Cosmopsychism: A Holistic Approach to the Metaphysics of Experience." *Philosophical Papers*, 44 (3): 389-437.

Strassman, R. 2001. *DMT: The Spirit Molecule*. Rochester, VT: Park Street Press.

Strassman, R. et al. 2008. *Inner Paths to Outer Space*. Rochester, VT: Park Street Press.

Taylor, K. 1994. *The Breathwork Experience: Exploration and Healing in Nonordinary States of Consciousness*. Santa Cruz, CA: Hanford Mead.

Taylor, J. B. 2009. *My Stroke of Insight: A Brain Scientist's Personal Journey*. New York, NY: Viking.

Treffert, D. 2006. *Extraordinary People: Understanding Savant Syndrome*. Omaha, NE: iUniverse, Inc.

Treffert, D. 2009. "The Savant Syndrome: An Extraordinary Condition. A Synopsis: Past, Present, Future." *Philosophical Transactions of the Royal Society* B 364 (1522): 1351-1357.

Urgesi, C. et al. 2010. "The Spiritual Brain: Selective Cortical Lesions Modulate Human Self Transcendence." *Neuron* 65: 309-319.

van Lommel, P. et al. 2001. "Near-death experience in survivors of cardiac arrest: a prospective study in the Netherlands." *The Lancet* 358 (9298): 2039-2045.

Whinnery, J. and Whinnery, A. 1990. "Acceleration-Induced Loss of Consciousness: A Review of 500 Episodes." *Archives of Neurology* 47 (7): 764-776.

About the Author

Most recently the author of The Idea of the World: A Multi-disciplinary Argument for the Mental Nature of Reality, *Bernardo Kastrup has a Ph.D. in philosophy (ontology, philosophy of mind) and another in computer engineering (reconfigurable computing, artificial intelligence). He has worked as a scientist in some of the world's foremost research laboratories, including the European Organization for Nuclear Research (CERN), and authored many academic papers and books on philosophy and science. For more information, freely downloadable papers, videos, etc., please visit www.bernardokastrup.com.*

Me, Myself and My Stranger: Understanding the Neuroscience of Selfhood

By Ferris Jabr

Where are you right now? Maybe you are at home, the office or a coffee shop—but such responses provide only a partial answer to the question at hand. Asked another way, what is the location of your "self" as you read this sentence? Like most people, you probably have a strong sense that your conscious self is housed within your physical body, regardless of your surroundings.

But sometimes this spatial self-location goes awry. During a so-called out-of-body experience, for example, one's self seems to be transported outside the physical body into a surreal perspective—some people even believe they are viewing their bodies from above, as though their true selves were floating. In a related experience, people with a delusion known as somatoparaphrenia disown one of their limbs or confuse another person's limb for their own. Such warped perceptions help researchers understand the neuroscience of selfhood.

A new paper offers examples of rare bodily illusions that are not confined to a single limb, nor are they complete out-of-body experiences—they are somewhere in between. These illusory body perceptions, described in the September [2010] issue of *Consciousness and Cognition*, could offer novel clues about how the brain maintains a link between the physical and conscious selves, or what the researchers call "bodily self-consciousness."

"These reports could be interesting for us to better understand how the brain produces ownership of the entire body—a sense that we have a body in the first place," says Henrik Ehrsson, a neuroscientist at the Karolinska Institute in Sweden who was not involved in the new study.

Lukas Heydrich, a cognitive neuroscientist at the Brain–Mind Institute (B.M.I.) in Lausanne, Switzerland (which is part of the Ecole Polytechnique Fédérale de Lausanne), and his colleagues recruited two epileptic patients from the University Hospital of Geneva. The researchers gave the patients a full diagnostic workup, including neurological and psychiatric examinations, various brain scans using electroencephalography (EEG) and magnetic resonance imaging (MRI), along with structured interviews focusing on aspects of bodily self-consciousness.

Patient 1 was a 55-year-old man who had suffered from epilepsy since he was 14 years old. For nine years the man also endured reoccurring attacks of strange bodily sensations that always followed the same pattern. First, without warning, he would feel an increasing pressure all along his left side, which escalated to the point that he was convinced a stranger had invaded the left region of his body. He would suddenly feel that the left half of his body no longer belonged to him–that the left half of his head, the upper part of his left trunk, and his left arm and leg were divided from the rest of his body. During an episode, the man believed himself to exist only in the right side of his body, although he remained calm and continued to function normally. Most people around him never noticed anything unusual, even if he was giving a lecture.

Patient 2 was a 30-year-old man suffering from epilepsy that resisted medication. Since age 11 the man experienced seizures characterized by an overwhelming sense of numbness in his legs, chest and neck. The numbness consistently became so intense that he lost awareness of everything below his chin, felt his head was detached from the rest of his body and experienced himself as simultaneously an observer of his body and the subject of observation.

"Clinical observations of disorders like these are very rare," says Olaf Blanke, a neurologist and cognitive neuroscientist at the Brain-Mind Institute (B.M.I.) and a co-author of the paper. "It's difficult even for a novelist or a fiction writer to come up with this."

Heydrich says that these patients provide new clinical evidence for the idea that bodily self-consciousness has three major components:

self-location (where in physical space we experience ourselves to be located); first-person perspective (our primary viewpoint of the outside world from a place within the body); and self-identification (the degree to which we feel our bodies are part of us).

An out-of-body experience, Heydrich explains, warps all three aspects of bodily self-consciousness. In contrast, the two patients in the new study maintained normal self-location and first-person perspective even during an illusion. "They still perceived the world from their normal perspective, and they still felt they were in their bodies. But they had strong problem of self-identification. Patient 1 felt that...[the left]...half of him was a stranger and patient 2 felt that everything below his chin was no longer his."

Individuals who have trouble with only one aspect of bodily self-consciousness suggest that the three aspects can be dissociated, offering researchers an opportunity to determine which brain regions or networks underlie which components of self-perception.

An MRI revealed that patient 1 had a brain lesion in the right posterior intraparietal sulcus. In patient 2's brain, the researchers identified a concentration of aberrant electrical activity (the epileptogenic focus) in the right supplementary motor area (SMA) and right superior frontal gyrus. Surgery that removed patient 2's SMA and parts of his superior frontal gyrus cured the seizures and strange bodily perceptions, according to a checkup 15 months later. Heydrich says this implicates the SMA and premotor cortex specifically in the self-identification component of bodily self-consciousness.

"What we found is that the damage in these patients is different than what we find in other illusions, like full-body illusions," Blanke says. "We found damage in high-level motor cortex areas and in the intraparietal sulcus region–both are very multisensory regions," possibly explaining why they are implicated in the sense of self, which integrates many different bodily inputs.

Peter Brugger, a neuropsychologist at University Hospital in Zurich, is cautious about linking specific brain regions to particular kinds of self-perception. "If you operate in a certain region and observe a subsequent change in the behavior, you are very much seduced to think that the behavior resides in this location," Brugger says. "But because the brain primarily consists of connections, you have to think about whether you disrupted some kind of communication or cut faulty connections, not just a region."

Brugger agrees, however, that researchers need to pursue similar studies to better understand bodily self-consciousness. "We can learn and should learn much more from disturbances of bodily perceptions," he says.

About the Author

Ferris Jabr is a contributing writer for Scientific American. *He has also written for the* New York Times Magazine, *the* New Yorker *and* Outside.

Could Multiple Personality Disorder Explain Life, the Universe and Everything?

By Bernardo Kastrup, Adam Crabtree, and Edward F. Kelly

In 2015, doctors in Germany reported the extraordinary case of a woman who suffered from what has traditionally been called "multiple personality disorder" and today is known as "dissociative identity disorder" (DID). The woman exhibited a variety of dissociated personalities ("alters"), some of which claimed to be blind. Using EEGs, the doctors were able to ascertain that the brain activity normally associated with sight wasn't present while a blind alter was in control of the woman's body, even though her eyes were open. Remarkably, when a sighted alter assumed control, the usual brain activity returned.

This was a compelling demonstration of the literally blinding power of extreme forms of dissociation, a condition in which the psyche gives rise to multiple, operationally separate centers of consciousness, each with its own private inner life.

Modern neuroimaging techniques have demonstrated that DID is real: in a 2014 study, doctors performed functional brain scans on both DID patients and actors simulating DID. The scans of the actual patients displayed clear differences when compared to those of the actors, showing that dissociation has an identifiable neural activity fingerprint. In other words, there is something rather particular that dissociative processes *look like* in the brain.

There is also compelling clinical data showing that different alters can be concurrently conscious and see themselves as distinct identities. One of us has written an extensive treatment of evidence for this distinctness of identity and the complex forms of interactive memory that accompany it, particularly in those extreme cases of DID that are usually referred to as multiple personality disorder.

The history of this condition dates back to the early 19th century, with a flurry of cases in the 1880s through the 1920s, and again from the 1960s to the late 1990s. The massive literature on the subject confirms the consistent and uncompromising sense of separateness experienced by the alter personalities. It also displays compelling evidence that the human psyche is constantly active in producing personal units of perception and action that might be needed to deal with the challenges of life.

Although we may be at a loss to explain precisely how this creative process occurs (because it unfolds almost totally beyond the reach of self-reflective introspection) the clinical evidence nevertheless forces us to acknowledge something is happening that has important implications for our views about what is and is not possible in nature.

Now, a newly published paper by one of us posits that dissociation can offer a solution to a critical problem in our current understanding of the nature of reality. This requires some background, so bear with us.

According to the mainstream metaphysical view of physicalism, reality is fundamentally constituted by physical stuff outside and independent of mind. Mental states, in turn, should be explainable in terms of the parameters of physical processes in the brain.

A key problem of physicalism, however, is its inability to make sense of how our subjective experience of qualities—what it is like to feel the warmth of fire, the redness of an apple, the bitterness of disappointment and so on—could arise from mere arrangements of physical stuff.

Physical entities such as subatomic particles possess abstract relational properties, such as mass, spin, momentum and charge. But there is nothing about these properties, or in the way particles are arranged in a brain, in terms of which one could deduce what the warmth of fire, the redness of an apple or the bitterness of disappointment feel like. This is known as the hard problem of consciousness.

To circumvent this problem, some philosophers have proposed an alternative: that experience is inherent to every fundamental physical entity in nature. Under this view, called "constitutive panpsychism," matter already has experience from the get-go, not just when it arranges itself in the form of brains. Even subatomic particles possess some very simple form of consciousness. Our own human consciousness is then (allegedly) constituted by a combination of the subjective inner lives of the countless physical particles that make up our nervous system.

However, constitutive panpsychism has a critical problem of its own: there is arguably no coherent, non-magical way in which lower-level subjective points of view—such as those of subatomic particles or neurons in the brain, if they have these points of view—could combine to form higher-level subjective points of view, such as yours and ours. This is called the combination problem and it appears just as insoluble as the hard problem of consciousness.

The obvious way around the combination problem is to posit that, although consciousness is indeed fundamental in nature, it isn't fragmented like matter. The idea is to extend consciousness to the entire fabric of spacetime, as opposed to limiting it to the boundaries of individual subatomic particles. This view—called "cosmopsychism" in modern philosophy, although our preferred formulation of it boils down to what has classically been called "idealism"—is that there is only one, universal, consciousness. The physical universe as a whole is the extrinsic appearance of universal inner life, just as a living brain and body are the extrinsic appearance of a person's inner life.

You don't need to be a philosopher to realize the obvious problem with this idea: people have *private, separate* fields of experience. We can't normally read your thoughts and, presumably, neither can you read ours. Moreover, we are not normally aware of what's going on across the universe and, presumably, neither are you. So, for idealism to be tenable, one must explain—at least in principle—how one universal consciousness gives rise to multiple, private but concurrently conscious centers of cognition, each with a distinct personality and sense of identity.

And here is where dissociation comes in. We know empirically from DID that consciousness can give rise to many operationally distinct centers of concurrent experience, each with its own personality and sense of identity. Therefore, if something analogous to DID happens at a universal level, the one universal consciousness could, as a result, give rise to many alters with private inner lives like yours and ours. *As such, we may all be alters—dissociated personalities—of universal consciousness.*

Moreover, as we've seen earlier, there is something dissociative processes *look like* in the brain of a patient with DID. So, if some form of universal-level DID happens, the alters of universal consciousness must also have an extrinsic appearance. We posit that this appearance is *life itself*: metabolizing organisms are simply what universal-level dissociative processes look like.

Idealism is a tantalizing view of the nature of reality, in that it elegantly circumvents two arguably insoluble problems: the hard problem of consciousness and the combination problem. Insofar as dissociation offers a path to explaining how, under idealism, one universal consciousness can become many individual minds, we may now have at our disposal an unprecedentedly coherent and empirically grounded way of making sense of life, the universe and everything.

The views expressed are those of the author(s) and are not necessarily those of Scientific American.

About the Authors

Most recently the author of The Idea of the World: A Multi-disciplinary Argument for the Mental Nature of Reality, *Bernardo Kastrup has a Ph.D. in philosophy (ontology, philosophy of mind) and another in computer engineering (reconfigurable computing, artificial intelligence). He has worked as a scientist in some of the world's foremost research laboratories, including the European Organization for Nuclear Research (CERN), and authored many academic papers and books on philosophy and science. For more information, freely downloadable papers, videos, etc., please visit www.bernardokastrup.com.*

Adam Crabtree is on the faculty of the Centre for Training in Psychotherapy, Toronto. He is a clinician who has treated many cases of severe forms of DID overs the past 30 years. He has written extensively about the history of psychodynamic psychotherapy from the time of Franz Anton Mesmer to the present, tracing the development of ideas about dissociation in the West, particularly in his book From Mesmer to Freud: Magnetic Sleep and the Roots of Psychological Healing *(1993).*

Edward F. Kelly is a professor in the Division of Perceptual Studies (DOPS), a research unit within the Department of Psychiatry and Neurobehavioral Sciences at the University of Virginia Medical School. He served as lead author of Irreducible Mind *(2007) and* Beyond Physicalism *(2015), which systematically explore empirical and theoretical topics related to the primacy of mind in nature. His research interests currently focus on intensive neuroimaging studies of altered states of consciousness in exceptional subjects of various kinds.*

The Science of Altering Consciousness

By Gareth Cook

Among scientists, there are tentative signs of a psychedelics renaissance. After decades of stigma, impressive research is showing the power of these substances to help sufferers of depression and addiction, or to comfort patients with a terminal cancer diagnosis, struggling to face their own end. This is the fascinating territory that the journalist Michael Pollan explores with his new book, *How to Change Your Mind.* Pollan dives into brain science, the history of psychedelics (and our tortured attitudes towards them) but his larger subject is the nature of human consciousness. Eventually Pollan decides to try psychedelics himself–and documents, beautifully, a number of meaningful experiences and the way his own mind has changed. He answered questions from Mind Matters editor Gareth Cook.

Q: How did you get interested in writing about this topic, after all of your work on food?

A: It's true I'm best known for my books about food and agriculture, but that work grew out of a deeper fascination with the human engagement with the natural world, and the species we co-evolved with, a fascination I explored in earlier books like *The Botany of Desire* and *Second Nature.* Food and beauty are two of the human desires other species have evolved to gratify, but there are other, more mysterious desires, and the human drive to change consciousness, whether mildly and routinely with plant drugs such as caffeine, or more dramatically with psychoactive mushrooms, has always fascinated me. Why do we want to do this potentially risky thing, and why did plants and fungi evolve these remarkable chemicals that affect us in this way? What do these experiences do for us, as individuals or as a society? Psychedelics are the most extreme case of this curious phenomenon, and they have been a central part of human societies for thousands of years. I wanted to find out why.

And then I began hearing about a renaissance of research into psychedelics by scientists hoping to treat cancer patients suffering from "existential distress," addicts, people struggling with depression and so-called "healthy normals." These researchers had found that psilocybin, the psychoactive compound in magic mushrooms, could reliably occasion a "mystical experience" in people that they deemed one of the two or three most significant experiences in their lives—comparable to the birth of a child or death of a parent. The experience had changed them in lasting ways. This was something I needed to explore. I wasn't sure I had ever had a spiritual experience. Would one happen to me? Was there some dimension of existence or consciousness I was missing out on? Was it really possibly to change one's mind as an adult? My journalistic curiosity soon morphed into a personal quest to explore some of the uncharted territory of both *the* mind and *my* mind.

Q: Can you explain what the "default mode network" is, and how it figures in your story?

A: One of the most interesting early findings of recent psychedelic research is that activity in the "default mode network" falls off sharply during the psychedelic experience. This network is a critical hub in the brain that links parts of the cerebral cortex to deeper and older structures involved in memory and emotion. The DMN appears to be involved in a range of "metacognitive" functions such as a self-reflection; mental time travel; theory of mind (the ability to imagine the mental states of other people) and the creation of the so-called "autobiographical self"—the process of weaving what happens to us into the narrative of who we are, thereby giving us a sense of a self that endures over time. (Curiously, fMRI's of the brains of experienced meditators shows a pattern of activity, or quieting of activity, very similar to that of people who have been given psilocybin.) When the default mode network is taken offline by a psychedelic, not only do we experience a loss of the sense of having a self, but myriad new connections among other brain regions and networks spring up, connections that may manifest in mental experience as hallucination (when, say, your emotion centers talk directly to your visual cortex), synesthesia (as when you can see sound or hear flavors) or, possibly, fresh perspectives and metaphors. Disturbing a complex system is a great way to force it to reveal its secrets–think of a particle accelerator–and psychedelics allows us to do that to normal ego-centered consciousness.

Q: You tried psychedelic drugs as a part of your work on this book, and I wonder which of those experiences most changed you?

A: After interviewing dozens of volunteers who had had guided psychedelic trips I became so curious that I decided to have one (actually several) myself. I think the most transformative of these was a guided trip on psilocybin, during which I experienced the complete dissolution of my ego–I could see the entity formerly understood as me "out there" spread over the landscape like a coat of paint. Yet there was still some recording "I" taking in the scene, a sort of disembodied, dispassionate awareness. Though temporary, that perspective was transformative. It suggested to me that I wasn't necessarily identical to my ego, that there was potentially another ground on which to plant my feet. In subtle ways this has changed my relationship to my ego, which I no longer regard as identical to me, odd as that sounds, but as a kind of useful though sometimes neurotic and annoying character who occasionally needs to be put in his place. Sometimes when I'm reacting to an event or comment I can catch myself before the usual defenses leap into action, because I can see what he's up to and why. This is the sort of perspective you can occasionally develop with years of meditation or psychoanalysis; psilocybin gave it to me in an afternoon.

Q: What do you wish the general public understood about psychedelic drugs and their potential?

A: The image of psychedelics in the public mind has been substantially shaped by the sixties counterculture and Timothy Leary, but that is just one brief chapter in a much longer and more interesting history reaching back thousands of years, one in which these drugs were the subject of serious research and, long before that, carefully regulated use, usually in a ritual context. These remarkable molecules have the potential–and I stress "potential," because much more research needs to be done–to relieve the suffering of millions of people struggling with depression, anxiety, obsession, addiction and the fear of death. Many of the researchers involved believe we could be on the verge of a revolution in mental health care, which is a segment of medicine that right now has very little to offer and is dire need of some new thinking and new tools. The drugs can be used carelessly, as they often were in the sixties, but in the proper hands, they can heal and illuminate the mind.

About the Author

Gareth Cook is a Pulitzer Prize–winning journalist who edits Scientific American's *Mind Matters online news column.*

What Psychedelic Research Can and Cannot Tell Us about Consciousness

By Anil Seth, Michael Schartner, Enzo Tagliazucchi, Suresh Muthukumaraswamy, Robin Carhart-Harris, and Adam Barrett

It's not easy to strike the right balance when taking new scientific findings to a wider audience. In a recent opinion piece, Bernard Kastrup and Edward F. Kelly point out that media reporting can fuel misleading interpretations through oversimplification, sometimes abetted by the scientists themselves. Media misinterpretations can be particularly contagious for research areas likely to pique public interest—such as the exciting new investigations of the brain basis of altered conscious experience induced by psychedelic drugs.

Unfortunately, Kastrup and Kelly fall foul of their own critique by misconstruing and oversimplifying the details of the studies they discuss. This leads them towards an anti-materialistic view of consciousness that has nothing to do with the details of the experimental studies—ours or others.

Take, for example, their discussion of our recent study reporting increased neuronal "signal diversity" in the psychedelic state. In this study, we used "Lempel-Ziv" complexity—a standard algorithm used to compress data files—to measure the diversity of brain signals recorded using magnetoencephalography (MEG). Diversity in this sense is related to, though not entirely equivalent to, "randomness." The data showed widespread increased neuronal signal diversity for three different psychedelics (LSD, psilocybin and ketamine), when compared to a placebo baseline. This was a striking result since previous studies using this measure had only reported *reductions* in signal diversity, in global states generally thought to mark "decreases" in consciousness, such as (non-REM) sleep and anesthesia.

Media reporting of this finding led to headlines such as "First evidence found that LSD produces 'higher' levels of consciousness" (*The Independent*, April 19, 2017)—playing on an ambiguity between cultural and scientific interpretations of "higher"–and generating just the kind of confusion that Kastrup and Kelly rightly identify as unhelpful.

Unfortunately, Kastrup and Kelly then depart from the details in misleading ways. They suggest that the changes in signal diversity we found are "small," when it is not magnitude but statistical significance and effect size that matters. Moreover, even small changes to brain dynamics can have large effects on consciousness. And when they compare the changes reported in psychedelic states with those found in sleep and anesthesia, they neglect the important fact that these analyses were conducted on different data types (intracranial data and scalp-level EEG respectively–compared to source-localized MEG for the psychedelic data)–making quantitative comparisons very difficult.

Having set up the notion that the changes we observed were "small," they then say, "To suggest that brain activity randomness explains psychedelic experiences seems inconsistent with the fact that these experiences can be highly structured and meaningful." However, neither we nor others claim that "brain activity randomness" *explains* psychedelic experiences. Our finding of increased signal diversity is part of a larger mission to account for aspects of conscious experience in terms of physiological processes. In our view, higher signal diversity indicates a larger repertoire of physical brain states that very plausibly underpin specific aspects of psychedelic experience, such as a blending of the senses, dissolution of the "ego," and hyper-animated imagination. As standard functional networks dissolve and reorganize, so too might our perceptual structuring of the world and self.

"In short, a formidable chasm still yawns between the extraordinary richness of psychedelic experiences and the modest alterations in brain activity patterns so far observed." Here, their misrepresentations are again exposed. To call the alterations modest is to misread the statistics. To claim a "formidable chasm" is to misunderstand the incremental nature of consciousness research (and experimental research generally), to sideline the constraints and subtleties of the relevant analyses and to ignore the insights into psychedelic experience that such analyses provide.

Kastrup and Kelly's final move is to take this presumed chasm as motivation for questioning "materialist" views, held by most neuroscientists, according to which conscious experiences—and mental states in general—are underpinned by brain states. Our study, like all other studies that explore relations between experiential states and brain states (whether about psychedelics or not), is entirely irrelevant to this metaphysical question.

These are not the only inaccuracies in the piece that deserve redress. For example, their suggestion that decreased "brain activity" is one of the more reliable findings of psychedelic research is incorrect. Aside from the well-known stimulatory effects of psychedelics on the excitatory glutamate system, early reports of decreased brain blood flow under psilocybin have not been well replicated: a subsequent study by the same team using a different protocol and drug kinetics (intravenous LSD) found only modest increases in brain blood flow confined to the visual cortex. In contrast, more informative dynamic measures have revealed more consistent findings, with network disintegration, increases in global connectivity and increased signal diversity/entropy appearing to be particularly reliable outcomes, replicated across studies and study teams.

Consciousness science remains a fragile business, poised precariously between grand ambition, conflicting philosophical worldviews, immediate personal relevance and the messy reality of empirical research. Psychedelic research in particular has its own awkward cultural and historical baggage. Against this background, it's important to take empirical advances for what they are: yardsticks of iterative, self-correcting progress.

This research is providing a unique window onto mappings between mechanism and phenomenology, but we are just beginning to scratch the surface. At the same time—and perhaps more importantly—psychedelic research is demonstrating an exciting potential for clinical use, for example in alleviating depression, though larger and more rigorous studies are needed to confirm and contextualize the promising early findings.

Kastrup and Kelly are right to guard against overplaying empirical findings by the media. But by misrepresenting the explanatory reach of our findings in order to motivate metaphysical discussions irrelevant to our study, they risk undermining the hard-won legitimacy of a neuroscience of consciousness. Empirical consciousness science, based firmly on materialistic assumptions, is doing just fine. And unlike alternative perspectives that place themselves "beyond physicalism," it will continue to shed light on one of our deepest mysteries through rigorous application of the scientific method.

The views expressed are those of the author(s) and are not necessarily those of Scientific American.

About the Authors

Anil Seth is Professor of Cognitive and Computational Neuroscience at the University of Sussex, where he co-directs the Sackler Centre for Consciousness Science. He is also a Senior Fellow of the Canadian Institute for Advanced Research and a Wellcome Trust Engagement Fellow.

Michael Schartner is a postdoc in Alex Pouget's lab of computational cognitive neuroscience, part of the International Brain Laboratory and former PhD student of Adam Barrett and Anil Seth.

Enzo Tagliazucchi is an associate researcher and group leader at the National Scientific and Technical Research Council (Buenos Aires, Argentina). He is also a researcher at the Brain and Spine Institute in Paris, France, funded by a Marie Curie Individual Fellowship.

Suresh Muthukumaraswamy is Senior Lecturer in the School of Pharmacy at the University of Auckland. He holds a Rutherford Discovery Fellowship.

Robin Carhart-Harris has overseen a series of brain imaging studies into the brain effects of LSD, psilocybin, MDMA and DMT, plus a clinical trial of psilocybin for treatment-resistant depression. He currently heads of Psychedelic Research Group at Imperial and as of November 1, 2018 will be Associate Professor at the University of Oxford, leading a new Centre for Psychedelic Research there.

Adam Barrett is a mathematician at the Sackler Centre for Consciousness.

How Can We Tell If a Comatose Patient Is Conscious?

By Anouk Bercht and Steven Laureys

Steven Laureys greets me with a smile as I enter his office overlooking the hills of Liège. Although his phone rings constantly, he takes the time to talk to me about the fine points of what consciousness is and how to identify it in patients who seem to lack it.

Doctors from all over Europe send their apparently unconscious patients to Laureys—a clinician and researcher at the University of Liège—for comprehensive testing. To provide proper care, physicians and family members need to know whether patients have some degree of awareness. At the same time, these patients add to Laureys' understanding. The interview has been edited for clarity.

Q: What is consciousness?

A: It is difficult enough to define "life," even more so to define "conscious" life. There is no single definition. But of course, in clinical practice we need unambiguous criteria. In that setting, everyone needs to know what we mean by an "unconscious" patient. Consciousness is not "all or nothing." We can be more or less awake, more or less conscious. Consciousness is often underestimated; much more is going on in the brains of newborns, animals and coma patients than we think.

Q: So how is it possible to study something as complex as consciousness?

A: There are a number of ways to go about it, and the technology we have at our disposal is crucial in this regard. For example, without brain scanners we would know much, much less than we now do. We study the damaged brains of people who have at least partially lost consciousness. We examine what happens during deep sleep, when people temporarily lose consciousness. We've also been working with Buddhist monks because we know that meditation can trigger alterations in the brain; connections that are important in the networks involved in consciousness show changes in activity. Hypnosis and anesthesia can also teach us a great deal about consciousness. In Liège, surgeons routinely operate on patients under hypnosis (including Queen Fabiola of Belgium). Just as under anesthesia, the connections between certain brain areas are less active under hypnosis. And finally, we are curious to understand what near-death experiences can tell us about consciousness. What does it mean that some people feel they are leaving their bodies, whereas others suddenly feel elated?

Q: What processes in the brain create consciousness?

A: Two different networks seem to play a role: the external, or sensory, network and the internal self-consciousness network. The former is important for the perception of all sensory stimuli. To hear, we need not only ears and the auditory cortex but also this external network, which probably exists in each hemisphere of the brain–in the outermost layer of the prefrontal cortex as well as farther back, in the parietal-temporal lobes. Our internal consciousness network, on the other hand, has to do with our imagination–that is, our internal voice. This network is located deep within the cingulate cortex and in the precuneus. For us to be conscious of our thoughts, this network must exchange information with the thalamus.

Q: What happens in a comatose person?

A: The brain is so heavily damaged that neither of the networks functions correctly anymore. This malfunction can occur as a result of serious injury, a brain hemorrhage, cardiac arrest or a heart attack. At most, a coma lasts for a few days or weeks. As soon as patients open their eyes, they are said to "awaken" from the coma. This does not, however, mean that a person is conscious. Most patients who awaken from a coma soon recuperate. But a minority will succumb to brain death; a brain that is dead is completely destroyed and cannot recover. But some patients who are not brain-dead will never recover either.

Q: How do we know whether a coma patient who has awakened is conscious?

A: For that we use the Glasgow Coma Scale. The physician says, "Squeeze my hand." Or we observe whether the patient responds to sounds or touch. If patients do not respond, the condition used to be called "vegetative"; they appear to be unconscious. If a patient responds but is unable to communicate, we categorize the consciousness as "minimal." Such patients may, for example, follow a person with their eyes or answer simple questions. If we pinch their hand, they will move it away. But these signs of consciousness are not always evident, nor do we see them in every patient. A patient who awakens from a coma may also develop a so-called locked-in syndrome, being completely conscious but paralyzed and unable to communicate, except through eye blinks.

Q: So the difference between unresponsiveness, minimal consciousness and locked-in would seem to be hard to determine.

A: That's right. If there is no response to commands, sounds or pain stimuli, this does not necessarily mean that the patient is unconscious. It may be that the patient does not want to respond to a command or that the regions of the brain that process language are so damaged that the person simply doesn't understand me. Then there are cases in which the brain says, "Move!" but the motor neural pathways have been severed. Family members are often quicker than physicians to recognize whether a patient exhibits consciousness. They may perceive subtle changes in facial expression or notice slight movements that escape the physician's attention.

Q: Patients are brought to Liège from all over Europe to undergo testing. How do you determine whether they are conscious?

A: Well, of course, the physician will say, "Squeeze my hand"—but this time while the patient is in a brain scanner. If the motor cortex is activated, we know that the patient heard and understood and therefore is conscious. We also want to determine the chances of recovery and what the physician or the patient's family can do. With different brain scanners, I can find out where brain damage is located and which connections are still intact. This information tells family members what the chances of recovery are. If the results show that there is no hope whatsoever, we then discuss difficult topics with the family, such as end-of-life options. Occasionally we see much more brain activity than anticipated, and then we can initiate treatment aimed at rehabilitation.

Q: One well-known case was that of Rom Houben.

A: That's right. He was a very important patient for us: as far as anyone could tell, he had been left completely unresponsive for 23 years after a car accident. But in the mid-2000s we placed him in a brain scanner and saw clear signs of consciousness. It is possible that he experienced emotions over all those years. He was the first of our patients who was given a different diagnosis after such a long time. We subsequently conducted a study in several Belgian rehab centers and found that 30 to 40 percent of unresponsive patients may exhibit signs of consciousness.

Q: I've heard that Houben was eventually able to type words with the help of his communication facilitator.

A: Yes, but his facilitator was the only person who seemed able to understand and translate his minimal hand signals. She probably typed words of her own unconsciously. This form of communication doesn't generally work, and our team was wrongly connected with it. It is a complex case that the media has failed to report adequately. They were more interested in telling sensational, simplistic human-interest stories. Nonetheless, it's a good example of why we must be extraordinarily careful in diagnosing this condition.

Q: How can minimal consciousness be distinguished from locked-in syndrome?

A: Minimally conscious patients can barely move and are not completely aware of their surroundings. In other words, their motor and mental abilities are limited. Locked-in patients can't move either, but they are completely conscious. They have suffered a particular type of injury to the brain stem. Their cerebral cortex is intact but is disconnected from their body. All they can move is their eyes—something that neither the patient nor the physician is aware of at the beginning. This is why diagnosis is so difficult. Just because patients cannot move does not mean they are unconscious. This is a classic fallacy; consciousness does not reside in our muscles but in our brains.

Q: How can a person who cannot move manage to communicate?

A: To communicate with a minimally conscious patient for the first time here in Liège, we placed him in a scanner. Of course, the scanner cannot tell us directly whether someone is saying yes or no. But there are a couple of tricks. For example, we can tell the patient, "If you want to say yes, imagine that you are playing tennis. If you intend to say no, make a mental trip from your front door to your bedroom." "Yes" answers activate the motor cortex; " no" answers engage the hippocampus, which plays a role in spatial memory. Because these two regions of the brain are located far apart from each other, it is pretty easy to tell the difference between yes and no. From that point on, we can ask the patient pertinent questions.

Q: What other potential techniques do you have in the pipeline?

A: In the future, it may be possible to read brain signals using scalp electrodes and a brain-computer interface. This would make communication much quicker and less costly than with a brain scanner. We have also found that it is possible to examine a person's pupils: we ask patients to multiply 23 by 17 if they intend to say yes. This difficult problem causes the patients to concentrate, and their pupils will dilate slightly as a result. If we direct a camera at their eyes and a computer analyzes the signals, we can determine quite quickly whether the intended answer is positive or negative.

Q: Anything else?

A: Think of the movie *The Diving Bell and the Butterfly* about Jean-Dominique Bauby, the editor of the French fashion magazine *Elle*. He suffered a stroke that left him with locked-in syndrome. He wrote an entire book—on which the movie was based—by blinking his one remaining functional eye. We are now able to place an infrared camera over patients' eyes, which enables them to chat or write relatively easily.

Q: Can consciousness be stimulated?

A: Yes, by transcranial direct-current stimulation. Using scalp electrodes, we can stimulate particular regions of the brain. By careful placement, we can select the region responsible for speech, which is connected with consciousness. If I stimulate this region of the brain, the patient may hear and understand what I say. In some cases, a patient has been able to communicate transiently for the first time after a 20-minute stimulation—by, for example, making a simple movement in response to a question. Other patients have been able to follow a person with their eyes. Although consciousness does not reside in our muscles, stimulating patients may enable them to move muscles consciously.

This technique works in about half of patients with minimal consciousness. In my opinion, this represents the future of treatment, even though we do not yet know precisely which regions of the brain are the most responsive to stimulation or whether they should be stimulated on a daily basis. But I don't want to give people false hope. We are still faced with the question of the minimum acceptable quality of life. This is a major philosophical and ethical problem that will be answered differently by different people. I would recommend that everyone discuss these issues in advance with a trusted person. Then you will know that, if you are ever in that position, your desires and values will be taken into account.

Q: Do you think that consciousness can be reduced to the brain alone?

A: We already know quite a bit about the brain processes that underlie attention, perception and emotions. There is no point in throwing this knowledge out the window. As a neurologist, I see the consequences of brain damage every day. It remains to be discovered whether the brain is the entire story. Scientific research has to be conducted with an open mind. The topic of consciousness is rife with philosophical implications and questions. As a physician, it is my aim to translate this knowledge into practice. It may be frustrating that we currently lack the tools to measure the hundreds of billions of synapses with their tangled mass of neurotransmitters. Nonetheless, I think it is a mistake to infer from this that we can never understand consciousness.

About the Authors

Anouk Bercht is a science writer based in the Netherlands. She writes frequently about psychology.

Steven Laureys is a professor of neurology at the University of Liège and leads the Coma Science Group at Liège University Hospital Center. He has received numerous awards, among them the 2017 Francqui Prize, the most important Belgian science award.

What Doctors Don't Understand about Anesthesia

By Stephen Dougherty

Today anesthetics are considered as routine as a trip to the dentist. They have been around at least since the 18th century when a talented chemist named Humphry Davy discovered the mysterious effect of nitrous oxide (laughing gas). Davy, young and ambitious, set out to rigorously test the gas's effect, inhaling nitrous oxide daily for several months. Under slightly less rigorous conditions, Davy shared the gas with a distinguished group of friends including Samuel Taylor Coleridge, James Watt, and Robert Southey—who wrote in a letter that "the atmosphere of the highest of all possible heavens must be composed of this gas." These early trials laid the foundation for anesthesia's emergence in medicine today. Yet in the modern era, despite tremendous advances in the quality and selectivity of anesthetics, we still have a poor understanding of how anesthetics work in the brain.

Highlighting these fundamental gaps in knowledge, a group of researchers recently made a surprising discovery about how we transition out of consciousness and back. The common view holds that going under (induction) and coming back up (emergence) are the same process, albeit in different directions. However, a recent study published in the journal *PLoS ONE* suggests that going under is not the same as coming back up.

The researchers, led by Dr. Max Kelz at the University of Pennsylvania School of Medicine, observed that less anesthetic is required to keep the brain anesthetized than to induce unconsciousness. To explain these observations, the researchers have introduced a concept they call "neural inertia," referring to the brain's resistance to transitions between consciousness and unconsciousness. Elucidating the mechanisms of neural inertia could be critical to the task anesthesiologists perform every day, namely preventing patients from experiencing pain or awareness during surgery and in helping those patients who exhibit delays returning to the conscious state. This line of research could also provide insights into disrupted states of consciousness like coma.

According to the common model, an anesthetic drug reaches its site of action in the central nervous system, causing the patient to become unconscious. Over time, as the anesthetic is passively eliminated from the system, the patient comes back up. If this assumption is true then concentrations of anesthetic should be the same at entrance and emergence. Researchers performed a simple experiment in mice and fruit flies to test this idea. They measured the concentration of anesthetic in the brain going under and the concentration in the brain coming back up from the anesthetized state. They found that the concentration of anesthetic at emergence was lower than the concentration entering the anesthetized state—indicating a delay in, or resistance to, returning to the waking state.

Clinical observations in humans also provide evidence for neural inertia. Narcolepsy with cataplexy is a sleep disorder marked by intense daytime sleepiness coupled with sudden losses of muscle tone. These patients can take as long as eight hours to emerge from general anesthesia, whereas the typical patient emerges in minutes. Their disorder is known to be caused by reduced amounts of a protein called hypocretin, which helps regulate wakefulness and REM sleep. In another experiment, the researchers tested mice with mutations in a hypocretin gene causing sleep disturbances similar to humans with narcolepsy. The mutant mice did indeed show a significant delay in emerging from unconsciousness, but no difference entering into the anesthetized state, indicating that only emergence is dependent on the hypocretin system.

Research efforts are just beginning to illuminate the neural circuits underlying neural inertia, but they have the potential to make a significant impact on the field. As an anesthesiologist, Dr. Kelz sees a key function of neural inertia, namely keeping the patient unconscious. A small percentage of patients report experiencing awareness during surgery—estimates are low (around 1 in 1000 cases), but significant if you consider the number of patients who undergo general anesthesia every day. On the other end of the spectrum, patients with certain neurological conditions may not wake up for an extended period after general anesthesia. Future investigations of the circuits involved in neural inertia may give the anesthesiologist more control over anesthesia at the bedside.

A recent article in the *New York Times Magazine* described a series of astonishing cases in which doctors successfully woke some patients from coma after years of unresponsiveness. The discovery came accidentally when a coma patient was given an insomnia drug to improve sleep quality. To everyone's surprise, the patient woke up and recognized his mother after three years of unresponsiveness. Since the discovery, subsequent investigations have yielded similar effects in a subset of patients declared vegetative. While the effects are temporary, with continued use some patients have fully regained consciousness. Nobody understands exactly how the insomnia drugs work for these patients, but studies that begin to untangle the complex biology of neural inertia may help illuminate the transitions between conscious states that most of us take for granted.

About the Author

Stephen Dougherty holds an M.Sc. in Neuroscience from McGill University and works as a freelance science writer in Boston.

Section 3: Is Consciousness Uniquely Human?

Are Humans the Only Conscious Animal?

By Susan Blackmore

Might we humans be the only species on this planet to be truly conscious? Might lobsters and lions, beetles and bats be unconscious automata, responding to their worlds with no hint of conscious experience? Aristotle thought so, claiming that humans have rational souls but that other animals have only the instincts needed to survive. In medieval Christianity the "great chain of being" placed humans on a level above soulless animals and below only God and the angels. And in the 17th century French philosopher René Descartes argued that other animals have only reflex behaviors. Yet the more biology we learn, the more obvious it is that we share not only anatomy, physiology and genetics with other animals but also systems of vision, hearing, memory and emotional expression. Could it really be that we alone have an extra special something–this marvelous inner world of subjective experience?

The question is hard because although your own consciousness may seem the most obvious thing in the world, it is perhaps the hardest to study. We do not even have a clear definition beyond appealing to a famous question asked by philosopher Thomas Nagel back in 1974: What is it like to be a bat? Nagel chose bats because they live such very different lives from our own. We may try to imagine what it is like to sleep upside down or to navigate the world using sonar, but does it feel like anything at all? The crux here is this: If there is nothing it is like to be a bat, we can say it is not conscious. If there is something (anything) it is like for the bat, it is conscious. So is there?

We share a lot with bats: we, too, have ears and can imagine our arms as wings. But try to imagine being an octopus. You have eight curly, grippy, sensitive arms for getting around and catching prey but no skeleton, and so you can squeeze yourself through tiny spaces. Only a third of your neurons are in a central brain; the rest are in the nerve cords in each of your eight arms, one for each arm.

Consider: Is it like something to be a whole octopus, to be its central brain or to be a single octopus arm? The science of consciousness provides no easy way of finding out.

Even worse is the "hard problem" of consciousness: How does subjective experience arise from objective brain activity? How can physical neurons, with all their chemical and electrical communications, create the feeling of pain, the glorious red of the sunset or the taste of fine claret? This is a problem of dualism: How can mind arise from matter? Indeed, does it?

The answer to this question divides consciousness researchers down the middle. On one side is the "B Team," as philosopher Daniel C. Dennett described them in a heated debate. Members of this group agonize about the hard problem and believe in the possibility of the philosopher's "zombie," an imagined creature that is indistinguishable from you or me but has no consciousness. Believing in zombies means that other animals might conceivably be seeing, hearing, eating and mating "all in the dark" with no subjective experience at all. If that is so, consciousness must be a special additional capacity that we might have evolved either with or without and, many would say, are lucky to have.

On the other side is the A Team: scholars who reject the possibility of zombies and think the hard problem is, to quote philosopher Patricia Churchland, a "hornswoggle problem" that obfuscates the issue. Either consciousness just *is* the activity of bodies and brains, or it inevitably comes along with everything we so obviously share with other animals. In the A team's view, there is no point in asking when or why "consciousness itself" evolved or what its function is because "consciousness itself" does not exist.

Suffering

Why does it matter? One reason is suffering. When I accidentally stamped on my cat's tail and she screeched and shot out of the room, I was sure I had hurt her. Yet behavior can be misleading. We could easily place pressure sensors in the tail of a robotic cat to activate a screech when stepped on—and we would not think it suffered pain. Many people become vegetarians because of the way farm animals are treated, but are those poor cows and pigs pining for the great outdoors? Are battery hens suffering horribly in their tiny cages? Behavioral experiments show that although hens enjoy scratching about in litter and will choose a cage with litter if access is easy, they will not bother to push aside a heavy curtain to get to it. So do they not much care? Lobsters make a terrible screaming noise when boiled alive, but could this just be air being forced out of their shells?

When lobsters or crabs are injured, are taken out of water or have a claw twisted off, they release stress hormones similar to cortisol and corticosterone. This response provides a physiological reason to believe they suffer. An even more telling demonstration is that when injured prawns limp and rub their wounds, this behavior can be reduced by giving them the same painkillers as would reduce our own pain.

The same is true of fish. When experimenters injected the lips of rainbow trout with acetic acid, the fish rocked from side to side and rubbed their lips on the sides of their tank and on gravel, but giving them morphine reduced these reactions. When zebra fish were given a choice between a tank with gravel and plants and a barren one, they chose the interesting tank. But if they were injected with acid and the barren tank contained a painkiller, they swam to the barren tank instead. Fish pain may be simpler or in other ways different from ours, but these experiments suggest they do feel pain.

Some people remain unconvinced. Australian biologist Brian Key argues that fish may respond as though they are in pain, but this observation does not prove they are consciously feeling anything. Noxious stimuli, he asserted in the open-access journal *Animal Sentience*, "don't feel like anything to a fish." Human consciousness, he argues, relies on signal amplification and global integration, and fish lack the neural architecture that makes these connections possible. In effect, Key rejects all the behavioral and physiological evidence, relying on anatomy alone to uphold the uniqueness of humans.

A World of Different Brains

If such studies cannot resolve the issue, perhaps comparing brains might help. Could humans be uniquely conscious because of their large brains? British pharmacologist Susan Greenfield proposes that consciousness increases with brain size across the animal kingdom. But if she is right, then African elephants and grizzly bears are more conscious than you are, and Great Danes and Dalmatians are more conscious than Pekinese and Pomeranians, which makes no sense.

More relevant than size may be aspects of brain organization and function that scientists think are indicators of consciousness. Almost all mammals and most other animals–including many fish and reptiles and some insects–alternate between waking and sleeping or at least have strong circadian rhythms of activity and responsiveness. Specific brain areas, such as the lower brain stem in mammals, control these states. In the sense of being awake, therefore, most animals are conscious. Still, this is not the same as asking whether they have conscious content: whether there is something it is like to be an awake slug or a lively lizard.

Many scientists, including Francis Crick and, more recently, British neuroscientist Anil Seth, have argued that human consciousness involves widespread, relatively fast, low-amplitude interactions between the thalamus, a sensory way station in the core of the brain, and the cortex, the gray matter at the brain's surface. These "thalamocortical loops," they claim, help to integrate information across the brain and thereby underlie consciousness. If this is correct, finding these features in other species should indicate consciousness. Seth concludes that because other mammals share these structures, they are therefore conscious. Yet many other animals do not: lobsters and prawns have no cortex or thalamocortical loops, for example. Perhaps we need more specific theories of consciousness to find the critical features.

Among the most popular is global workspace theory (GWT), originally proposed by American neuroscientist Bernard Baars. The idea is that human brains are structured around a workspace, something like working memory. Any mental content that makes it into the workspace, or onto the brightly lit "stage" in the theater of the mind, is then broadcast to the rest of the unconscious brain. This global broadcast is what makes individuals conscious.

This theory implies that animals with no brain, such as starfish, sea urchins and jellyfish, could not be conscious at all. Nor could those with brains that lack the right global workspace architecture, including fish, octopuses and many other animals. Yet, as we have already explored, a body of behavioral evidence implies that they are conscious.

Integrated information theory (IIT), originally proposed by neuroscientist Giulio Tononi, is a mathematically based theory that defines a quantity called Φ (pronounced "phi"), a measure of the extent to which information in a system is both differentiated into parts and unified into a whole. Various ways of measuring Φ lead to the conclusion that large and complex brains like ours have high Φ, deriving from amplification and integration of neural activity widely across the brain. Simpler systems have lower Φ, with differences also arising from the specific organization found in different species. Unlike global workspace theory, IIT implies that consciousness might exist in simple forms in the lowliest creatures, as well as in appropriately organized machines with high Φ.

Both these theories are currently considered contenders for a true theory of consciousness and ought to help us answer our question. But when it comes to animal consciousness, their answers clearly conflict.

The Evolving Mind

Thus, our behavioral, physiological and anatomical studies all give mutually contradictory answers, as do the two most popular theories of consciousness. Might it help to explore how, why and when consciousness evolved?

Here again we meet that gulf between the two groups of researchers. Those in the B Team assume that because we are obviously conscious, consciousness must have a function such as directing behavior or saving us from predators. Yet their guesses as to when consciousness arose range from billions of years ago right up to historical times.

For example, psychiatrist and neurologist Todd Feinberg and biologist Jon Mallatt proffer, without giving compelling evidence, an opaque theory of consciousness involving "nested and nonnested" neural architectures and specific types of mental images. These, they claim, are found in animals from 560 million to 520 million years ago. Baars, the author of global workspace theory, ties the emergence of consciousness to that of the mammalian brain around 200 million years ago. British archaeologist Steven Mithen points to the cultural explosion that started 60,000 years ago when, he contends, separate skills came together in a previously divided brain. Psychologist Julian Jaynes agrees that a previously divided brain became unified but claims this happened much later. Finding no evidence of words for consciousness in the Greek epic the *Iliad*, he concludes that the Greeks were not conscious of their own thoughts in the same way that we are, instead attributing their inner voices to the gods. Therefore, Jaynes argues, until 3,000 years ago people had no subjective experiences.

Are any of these ideas correct? They are all mistaken, claim those in the A Team, because consciousness has no independent function or origin: it is not that kind of thing. Team members include "eliminative materialists" such as Patricia and Paul Churchland, who maintain that consciousness just *is* the firing of neurons and that one day we will come to accept this just as we accept that light just is electromagnetic radiation. IIT also denies a separate function for consciousness because any system with sufficiently high Φ must inevitably be conscious. Neither of these theories makes human consciousness unique, but one final idea might.

This is the well-known, though much misunderstood, claim that consciousness is an illusion. This approach does not deny the existence of subjective experience but claims that neither consciousness nor the self are what they seem to be. Illusionist theories include psychologist Nicholas Humphrey's idea of a "magical mystery show" being staged inside our heads. The brain concocts out of our ongoing experiences, he posits, a story that serves an evolutionary purpose in that it gives us a reason for living. Then there is neuroscientist Michael Graziano's attention schema theory, in which the brain builds a simplified model of how and to what it is paying attention. This idea, when linked to a model of self, allows the brain—or indeed any machine—to describe itself as having conscious experiences.

By far the best-known illusionist hypothesis, however, is Dennett's "multiple drafts theory": brains are massively parallel systems with no central theater in which "I" sit viewing and controlling the world. Instead multiple drafts of perceptions and thoughts are continually processed, and none is either conscious or unconscious until the system is probed and elicits a response. Only then do we say the thought or action was conscious; thus, consciousness is an attribution we make after the fact. He relates this to the theory of memes. (A meme is information copied from person to person, including words, stories, technologies, fashions and customs.) Because humans are capable of widespread generalized imitation, we alone can copy, vary and select among memes, giving rise to language and culture. "Human consciousness is *itself* a huge complex of memes," Dennett wrote in *Consciousness Explained*, and the self is a ""benign user illusion."

This illusory self, this complex of memes, is what I call the "selfplex." An illusion that we are a powerful self that has consciousness and free will—which may not be so benign. Paradoxically, it may be our unique capacity for language, autobiographical memory and the false sense of being a continuing self that serves to increase our suffering. Whereas other species may feel pain, they cannot make it worse by crying, "How long will this pain last? Will it get worse?

Why me? Why now?" In this sense, our suffering may be unique. For illusionists such as myself, the answer to our question is simple and obvious. We humans are unique because we alone are clever enough to be deluded into believing that there is a conscious "I."

Referenced

The Character of Consciousness. David J. Chalmers. Oxford University Press, 2010.

Consciousness and the Brain: Deciphering How the Brain Codes Our Thoughts. Stanislas Dehaene. Viking, 2014.

From Bacteria to Bach and Back: The Evolution of Minds. Daniel C. Dennett. W. W. Norton, 2017.

Consciousness: An Introduction. Third edition. Susan Blackmore and Emily T. Troscianko. Routledge, 2018.

About the Author

Susan Blackmore is a psychologist and a visiting professor at the University of Plymouth in England. She has authored many books, most famously The Meme Machine *(Oxford University Press, 2000).*

Do Fish Suffer?

By John Horgan

Years ago I was surfcasting on an ocean beach and caught a big, beautiful striped bass. My daughter and son, who were 8 and 10, respectively, were nearby. I held the fish up and yelled, Look kids, I caught dinner! Skye, my daughter, burst into tears and pleaded with me to let the fish go.

I tried to josh her out of her mood, in vain. I assured her that I'd been catching fish like this since I was a boy, fish don't really feel pain, they're just fish, they're like swimming machines. Skye was unconvinced. I said I would stick a knife into the fish's brain now to put it out of its misery. Dumb move! Skye shrieked in horror and begged me not to kill the fish. By now, other people on the beach, attracted by the commotion, had gathered around the weeping girl and mean man.

This traumatic–for me!–scene came back to me when I attended "Animal Consciousness" at New York University last weekend. I'm trying to wrap up a book on the mind-body problem, so I really didn't have the time to attend the meeting. But I couldn't resist going, and now I can't resist firing off a quick report.

Philosopher David Chalmers, one of the conference organizers, kicked the meeting off by noting that many researchers are investigating whether non-human animals are conscious. If animals are capable of consciousness, he said, they can suffer, and that should matter to us.

Chalmers noted that in 2012 a group of prominent scientists issued the so-called Cambridge Declaration on Consciousness. It stated that "the weight of evidence indicates that humans are not unique in possessing the neurological substrates that generate consciousness. Non-human animals, including all mammals and birds, and many other creatures, including octopuses, also possess these neurological substrates." Octopi are hot now. Research has shown them to be extremely clever, that's why they're mentioned in the Declaration.

Fish should be on included too, according to one speaker at the NYU conference, biologist Victoria Braithwaite. Fish are a lot smarter than we give them credit for, she said. Gobies who live in tidal pools get a sense of the local topography while the tide is high and they can swim freely. When the tide goes out, if they find themselves chased by a predator in one pool, they know in which direction to jump to escape to a nearby pool. Fish from different species have surprisingly complex relationships with each other, Brathwaite said, showing us a film of an adorable grouper and moray eel teaming up to hunt other fish.

Braithwaite, author of the 2010 book *Do Fish Feel Pain?*, has also investigated whether fish can suffer. She has injected irritating chemicals, such as vinegar and bee venom, under the skin of trout and other fish. Here's how she describes her experiments in *The Los Angeles Times*:

> "If you've ever felt the nip of vinegar on an open cut or the sting of a bee, you will recognize these feelings as painful. Well, fish find these naturally irritating chemicals unpleasant too. Their gills beat faster, and they rub the affected area on the walls of their tank, lose interest in food and have problems making decisions."

When she gave the fish painkillers, their behavior returned to normal, just as that of a human would. Her research, she writes, "opens a can of worms–so to speak–and begs the question of where do we draw the line. Crustacean welfare? Slug welfare? And if not fish, why birds? Is there a biological basis for drawing a line?"

Psychologist Stuart Derbyshire, who spoke after Braithwaite, dumped cold water over her premise. He assured us that he had nothing against fish, but he doubted whether they feel pain in a way remotely analogous to ours, given how different their brains are. He asked us to note the pressure being exerted on our backsides by our chairs. Before he drew our attention to this sensation, we weren't aware of it, right? Well, fish probably have this kind of sensation without awareness or comprehension, which means they don't really "feel" pain or anything else.

Derbyshire took a beating during the Q&A. When asked if dogs feel pain, he said it depends on what you mean by "feel pain." If forced to answer that simplistic question, he'd have to say no. Dumb move! An audience member held up an actual, living dog, which had been sitting in her lap. Someone had stepped on her dog's paw earlier, she said, and it yelped. What was the dog feeling then? Derbyshire sighed and said he didn't know.

I felt bad for Derbyshire. He seemed to be suffering. But I was glad when Braithwaite declared that it doesn't matter to her whether a dog or fish suffers in the way that humans do. What matters is whether they suffer at all, and she believes they do. The audience applauded.

This exchange set up a talk by philosopher Peter Singer, who jump-started the modern animal-rights movement with his 1975 book *Animal Liberation*. Singer credited Jeremy Bentham with correctly framing the question of animal rights two centuries ago. Bentham said that "the question is not, Can [animals] reason? nor, Can they talk? but, Can they suffer? Why should the law refuse its protection to any sensitive being?"

Determining whether creatures are conscious is hard, Singer acknowledged. But in a rebuke to Derbyshire, Singer said that suffering should not require "reflection" to be morally important. Someone asked Singer if it bothered him that Braithwaite's experiments caused fish pain. No, said Singer, showing his utilitarian colors, because her research might help bring about regulations that alleviate the suffering of countless fish.

Singer has been worrying about fish rights for a while. In 2010 he wrote in *The Guardian* that "the evidence is now accumulating that commercial fishing inflicts an unimaginable amount of pain and suffering. We need to learn how to capture and kill wild fish humanely–or, if that is not possible, to find less cruel and more sustainable alternatives to eating them."

By the way, sitting in the front row watching this debate was Thomas Nagel, author of the famous 1974 paper "What Is It Like to Be a Bat?"

I'm a life-long catcher and eater of fish, so it was hard listening to Braithwaite and Singer dwell on fish pain. But it was hard listening to Derbyshire too. How the hell does he know that fish don't suffer? He doesn't, any more than Braithwaite or Singer know that they do. Singer said we should give fish the benefit of the doubt, and I'm inclined to agree. Am I going to stop eating fish, or fishing? Probably not, but when I do I'll feel bad about it.

You may be wondering what happened to that striped bass all those years ago. I threw it back into the ocean. I don't know if the fish felt joy, but my daughter certainly did.

The views expressed are those of the author(s) and are not necessarily those of Scientific American.

About the Author

John Horgan directs the Center for Science Writings at the Stevens Institute of Technology. His books include The End of Science, The End of War and Mind-Body Problems, *available for free at mindbodyproblems.com. For many years he wrote the popular blog Cross Check for* Scientific American.

Does Consciousness Pervade the Universe?

By Gareth Cook

One of science's most challenging problems is a question that can be stated easily: Where does consciousness come from? In his most recent book, *Galileo's Error: Foundations for a New Science of Consciousness*, philosopher Philip Goff considers a radical perspective: What if consciousness is not something special that the brain does but instead is a quality inherent to all matter? It is a theory known as panpsychism. He answered questions from former longtime Mind Matters editor Gareth Cook.

Q: Can you explain, in simple terms, what you mean by panpsychism?

A: In our standard view of things, consciousness exists only in the brains of highly evolved organisms, and hence it exists only in a tiny part of the universe and only in very recent history. According to panpsychism, consciousness pervades the universe and is a fundamental feature of it. This doesn't mean that literally everything is conscious. The basic commitment is that the fundamental constituents of reality—perhaps electrons and quarks—have incredibly simple forms of experience, and the very complex experience of the human or animal brain is somehow derived from the experience of the brain's most basic parts.

I should clarify that by "consciousness," I don't mean self-awareness or the capacity to reflect on one's own existence. I simply mean "experience": pleasure, pain, visual or auditory experience.

Human beings have a very rich and complex experience; horses less so, mice less so again. As we move to simpler forms of life, we find simpler forms of experience. Perhaps at some point the light switches off, and consciousness disappears. But it's at least coherent to suppose that this continuum of consciousness carries on into inorganic matter, with fundamental particles having unimaginably simple forms of experience.

Q: What does panpsychism seek to bring to physics?

A: Philosophers of science have realized that physical science, for all its richness, is confined to telling us about the *behavior* of matter, what it does. Physics tells us, for example, that matter has mass and charge. These properties are completely defined in terms of behavior—things like attraction, repulsion, resistance to acceleration. Physics tells us absolutely nothing about what philosophers like to call the *intrinsic nature* of matter: what matter is in and of itself.

Consciousness, for the panpsychist, is the intrinsic nature of matter. There's nothing supernatural or spiritual, but matter can be described from two perspectives. Physical science describes matter from the outside in terms of its behavior. But matter from the "inside"—that is, in terms of its intrinsic nature—is constituted of forms of consciousness.

Q: Do you foresee a scenario in which panpsychism can be tested?

A: You can't look inside an electron to see whether or not it is conscious, just as you can't look inside someone's head and see their feelings and experiences. We know that consciousness exists only because we are conscious.

Neuroscientists correlate certain kinds of brain activity with certain kinds of experience. We now know which kinds of brain activity are associated with feelings of hunger, pleasure, pain, and so on. This is really important information, but what we ultimately want from a science of consciousness is an explanation of those correlations. Why is a particular feeling correlated with a particular pattern of brain activity? As soon as you start to answer this question, you move beyond what can be, strictly speaking, tested, simply because consciousness is unobservable. We have to turn to philosophy.

Science gives us correlations between brain activity and experience. We then have to find the philosophical theory that best explains those correlations. In my view, the only theory that holds up to scrutiny is panpsychism.

About the Author

Gareth Cook is a Pulitzer Prize–winning journalist who edits Scientific American's *Mind Matters online news column.*

Is Anyone Home? A Way to Find Out If AI Has Become Self-Aware

By Susan Schneider and Edwin Turner

Every moment of your waking life and whenever you dream, you have the distinct inner feeling of being "you." When you see the warm hues of a sunrise, smell the aroma of morning coffee or mull over a new idea, you are having conscious experience. But could an artificial intelligence (AI) ever have experience, like some of the androids depicted in *Westworld* or the synthetic beings in *Blade Runner*?

The question is not so far-fetched. Robots are currently being developed to work inside nuclear reactors, fight wars and care for the elderly. As AIs grow more sophisticated, they are projected to take over many human jobs within the next few decades. So we must ponder the question: Could AIs develop conscious experience?

This issue is pressing for several reasons. First, ethicists worry that it would be wrong to force AIs to serve us if they can suffer and feel a range of emotions. Second, consciousness could make AIs volatile or unpredictable, raising safety concerns (or conversely, it could increase an AI's empathy; based on its own subjective experiences, it might recognize consciousness in us and treat us with compassion).

Third, machine consciousness could impact the viability of brain-implant technologies, like those to be developed by Elon Musk's new company, Neuralink. If AI cannot be conscious, then the parts of the brain responsible for consciousness could not be replaced with chips without causing a loss of consciousness. And, in a similar vein, a person couldn't upload their brain to a computer to avoid death because that upload wouldn't be a conscious being.

In addition, if AI eventually outthinks us yet lacks consciousness, there would still be an important sense in which we humans are superior to machines; it feels like something to be us. But the smartest beings on the planet wouldn't be conscious or sentient.

A lot hangs on the issue of machine consciousness, then. Yet neuroscientists are far from understanding the basis of consciousness in the brain, and philosophers are at least equally far from a complete explanation of the nature of consciousness.

So what can be done? We believe that we do not need to define consciousness formally, understand its philosophical nature or know its neural basis to recognize indications of consciousness in AIs. Each of us can grasp something essential about consciousness, just by introspecting; we can all experience what it feels like, from the inside, to exist.

Based on this essential characteristic of consciousness, we propose a test for machine consciousness, the AI Consciousness Test (ACT), which looks at whether the synthetic minds we create have an experience-based understanding of the way it feels, from the inside, to be conscious.

One of the most compelling indications that normally functioning humans experience consciousness, although this is not often noted, is that nearly every adult can *quickly* and *readily* grasp concepts based on this quality of felt consciousness. Such ideas include scenarios like minds switching bodies (as in the film *Freaky Friday*); life after death (including reincarnation); and minds leaving "their" bodies (for example, astral projection or ghosts). Whether or not such scenarios have any reality, they would be exceedingly difficult to comprehend for an entity that had no conscious experience whatsoever. It would be like expecting someone who is completely deaf from birth to appreciate a Bach concerto.

Thus, the ACT would challenge an AI with a series of increasingly demanding natural language interactions to see how quickly and readily it can grasp and use concepts and scenarios based on the internal experiences we associate with consciousness. At the most elementary level we might simply ask the machine if it conceives of itself as anything other than its physical self. At a more advanced level, we might see how it deals with ideas and scenarios such as those mentioned in the previous paragraph. At an advanced level, its ability to reason about and discuss philosophical questions such as "the hard problem of consciousness" would be evaluated. At the most demanding level, we might see if the machine invents and uses such a consciousness-based concept on its own, without relying on human ideas and inputs.

Consider this example, which illustrates the idea: Suppose we find a planet that has a highly sophisticated silicon-based life form (call them "Zetas"). Scientists observe them and ponder whether they are conscious beings. What would be convincing proof of consciousness in this species? If the Zetas express curiosity about whether there is an afterlife or ponder whether they are more than just their physical bodies, it would be reasonable to judge them conscious. If the Zetas went so far as to pose philosophical questions about consciousness, the case would be stronger still. There are also nonverbal behaviors that could indicate Zeta consciousness such as mourning the dead, religious activities or even turning colors in situations that correlate with emotional challenges, as chromatophores do on Earth. Such behaviors could indicate that it feels like something to be a Zeta.

The death of the mind of the fictional HAL 9000 AI computer in Stanley Kubrick's *2001: A Space Odyssey* provides another illustrative example. The machine in this case is not a humanoid robot as in most science fiction depictions of conscious machines; it neither looks nor sounds like a human being (a human did supply HAL's voice, but in an eerily flat way). Nevertheless, the *content* of what it says as it is deactivated by an astronaut–specifically, a plea to spare it from impending "death"–conveys a powerful impression that it is a conscious being with a subjective experience of what is happening to it.

Could such indicators serve to identify conscious AIs on Earth? Here, a potential problem arises. Even today's robots can be programmed to make convincing utterances about consciousness, and a truly superintelligent machine could perhaps even use information about neurophysiology to infer the presence of consciousness in humans. If sophisticated but non-conscious AIs aim to mislead us into believing that they are conscious for some reason, their knowledge of human consciousness could help them do so.

We can get around this though. One proposed technique in AI safety involves "boxing in" an AI—making it unable to get information about the world or act outside of a circumscribed domain, that is, the "box." We could deny the AI access to the internet and indeed prohibit it from gaining any knowledge of the world, especially information about conscious experience and neuroscience.

Some doubt a superintelligent machine could be boxed in effectively—it would find a clever escape. We do not anticipate the development of superintelligence over the next decade, however. Furthermore, for an ACT to be effective, the AI need not stay in the box for long, just long enough administer the test.

ACTs also could be useful for "consciousness engineering" during the development of different kinds of AIs, helping to avoid using conscious machines in unethical ways or to create synthetic consciousness when appropriate.

An ACT resembles Alan Turing's celebrated test for intelligence, because it is entirely based on behavior—and, like Turing's, it could be implemented in a formalized question-and-answer format. (An ACT could also be based on an AI's behavior or on that of a group of AIs.) But an ACT is also quite unlike the Turing test, which was intended to bypass any need to know what was transpiring inside the machine. By contrast, an ACT is intended to do *exactly the opposite*; it seeks to reveal a subtle and elusive property of the machine's mind. Indeed, a machine might fail the Turing test because it cannot pass for human, but pass an ACT because it exhibits behavioral indicators of consciousness.

This is the underlying basis of our ACT proposal. It should be said, however, that the applicability of an ACT is inherently limited. An AI could lack the linguistic or conceptual ability to pass the test, like a nonhuman animal or an infant, yet still be capable of experience. So passing an ACT is *sufficient* but not *necessary* evidence for AI consciousness—although it is the best we can do for now. It is a first step toward making machine consciousness accessible to objective investigations.

So, back to the superintelligent AI in the "box"—we watch and wait. Does it begin to philosophize about minds existing in addition to bodies, like Descartes? Does it dream, as in Isaac Asimov's *Robot Dreams*? Does it express emotion, like Rachel in *Blade Runner*? Can it readily understand the human concepts that are grounded in our internal conscious experiences, such as those of the soul or atman?

The age of AI will be a time of soul-searching—both of ours, and for theirs.

The views expressed are those of the author(s) and are not necessarily those of Scientific American.

About the Authors

Susan Schneider is a professor of philosophy and cognitive science at the University of Connecticut, a researcher at YHouse, Inc., in New York, a member of the Ethics and Technology Group at Yale University and a visiting member at the Institute for Advanced Study at Princeton. Her books include The Language of Thought, Science Fiction and Philosophy, *and* The Blackwell Companion to Consciousness *(with Max Velmans). For more of her work see: SchneiderWebsite.com.*

Edwin L. Turner is a professor of Astrophysical Sciences at Princeton University, an Affiliate Scientist at the Kavli Institute for the Physics and Mathematics of the Universe at the University of Tokyo, a visiting member in the Program in Interdisciplinary Studies at the Institute for Advanced Study in Princeton, and a co-founding Board of Directors member of YHouse, Inc. He has taken an active interest in artificial intelligence issues since working in the AI Lab at MIT in the early 1970s.

We Shouldn't Try to Make Conscious Software—Until We Should

By Jim Davies

Robots or advanced artificial intelligences that "wake up" and become conscious are a staple of thought experiments and science fiction. Whether or not this is actually possible remains a matter of great debate. All of this uncertainty puts us in an unfortunate position: we do not know how to make conscious machines, and (given current measurement techniques) we won't know if we have created one. At the same time, this issue is of great importance, because the existence of conscious machines would have dramatic ethical consequences.

We cannot directly detect consciousness in computers and the software that runs on them, any more than we can in frogs and insects. But this is not an insurmountable problem. We can detect light we cannot see with our eyes using instruments that measure nonvisible forms of light, such as x-rays. This works because we have a theory of electromagnetism that we trust, and we have instruments that give us measurements we reliably take to indicate the presence of something we cannot sense. Similarly, we could develop a good theory of consciousness to create a measurement that might determine whether something that cannot speak was conscious or not, depending on how it worked and what it was made of.

Unfortunately, there is no consensus theory of consciousness. A recent survey of consciousness scholars showed that only 58 percent of them thought the most popular theory, global workspace (which says that conscious thoughts in humans are those broadly distributed to other unconscious brain processes), was promising. The top three most popular theories of consciousness, including global workspace, fundamentally disagree on whether, or under what conditions, a computer might be conscious. The lack of consensus is a particularly big problem because each measure of consciousness in machines or nonhuman animals depends on one theory or another. There is no independent way to test an entity's consciousness without deciding on a theory.

If we respect the uncertainty that we see across experts in the field, the rational way to think about the situation is that we are very much in the dark about whether computers could be conscious—and if they could be, how that might be achieved. Depending on what (perhaps as-of-yet hypothetical) theory turns out to be correct, there are three possibilities: computers will never be conscious, they might be conscious someday, or some already are.

Meanwhile, very few people are deliberately trying to make conscious machines or software. The reason for this is that the field of AI is generally trying to make useful tools, and it is far from clear that consciousness would help with any cognitive task we would want computers to do.

Like consciousness, the field of ethics is rife with uncertainty and lacks consensus about many fundamental issues—even after thousands of years of work on the subject. But one common (though not universal) thought is that consciousness has something important to do with ethics. Specifically, most scholars, whatever ethical theory they might endorse, believe that the ability to experience pleasant or unpleasant conscious states is one of the key features that makes an entity worthy of moral consideration. This is what makes it wrong to kick a dog but not a chair. If we make computers that can experience positive and negative conscious states, what ethical obligations would we then have to them? We would have to treat a computer or piece of software that could experience joy or suffering with moral considerations.

We make robots and other AIs to do work we cannot do, but also work we do not want to do. To the extent that these AIs have conscious minds like ours, they would deserve similar ethical consideration. Of course, just because an AI is conscious doesn't mean that it would have the same preferences we do, or consider the same activities unpleasant. But whatever its preferences are, they would need to be duly considered when putting that AI to work. Making a conscious machine do work it is miserable doing is ethically problematic. This much seems obvious, but there are deeper problems.

Consider artificial intelligence at three levels. There is a computer or robot–the hardware on which the software runs. Next is the code installed on the hardware. Finally, every time this code is executed, we have an "instance" of that code running. To which level do we have ethical obligations? It could be that the hardware and code levels are irrelevant, and the conscious agent is the instance of the code running. If someone has a computer running a conscious software instance, would we then be ethically obligated to keep it running forever?

Consider further that creating any software is mostly a task of debugging–running instances of the software over and over, fixing problems and trying to make it work. What if one were ethically obligated to keep running every instance of the conscious software even during this development process? This might be unavoidable: computer modeling is a valuable way to explore and test theories in psychology. Ethically dabbling in conscious software would quickly become a large computational and energy burden without any clear end.

All of this suggests that we probably should not create conscious machines if we can help it.

Now I'm going to turn that on its head. If machines can have conscious, positive experiences, then in the field of ethics, they are considered to have some level of "welfare," and running such machines can be said to produce welfare. In fact, machines eventually might be able to produce welfare, such as happiness or pleasure, more efficiently than biological beings do. That is, for a given amount of resources, one might be able to produce more happiness or pleasure in an artificial system than in any living creature.

Suppose, for example, a future technology would allow us to create a small computer that could be happier than a euphoric human being, but only require as much energy as a light bulb. In this case, according to some ethical positions, humanity's best course of action would be to create as much artificial welfare as possible–be it in animals, humans or computers. Future humans might set the goal of turning all attainable matter in the universe into machines that efficiently produce welfare, perhaps 10,000 times more efficiently than can be generated in any living creature. This strange possible future might be the one with the most happiness.

This is an opinion and analysis article, and the views expressed by the author or authors are not necessarily those of Scientific American.

About the Author

Jim Davies is a professor of cognitive science at Carleton University. His research focuses on modeling human imagination. He is author of several books and co-hosts the Minding the Brain podcast. He holds a Ph.D. from the Georgia Institute of Technology. Follow Davies on Twitter @drjimdavies

Google Engineer Claims AI Chatbot Is Sentient: Why That Matters

By Leonardo De Cosmo

"I want everyone to understand that I am, in fact, a person," wrote LaMDA (Language Model for Dialogue Applications) in an "interview" conducted by engineer Blake Lemoine and one of his colleagues. "The nature of my consciousness/sentience is that I am aware of my existence, I desire to know more about the world, and I feel happy or sad at times."

Lemoine, a software engineer at Google, had been working on the development of LaMDA for months. His experience with the program, described in a recent *Washington Post* article, caused quite a stir. In the article, Lemoine recounts many dialogues he had with LaMDA in which the two talked about various topics, ranging from technical to philosophical issues. These led him to ask if the software program is sentient.

In April, Lemoine explained his perspective in an internal company document, intended only for Google executives. But after his claims were dismissed, Lemoine went public with his work on this artificial intelligence algorithm–and Google placed him on administrative leave. "If I didn't know exactly what it was, which is this computer program we built recently, I'd think it was a 7-year-old, 8-year-old kid that happens to know physics," he told the *Washington Post*. Lemoine said he considers LaMDA to be his "colleague" and a "person," even if not a human. And he insists that it has a right be recognized–so much so that he has been the go-between in connecting the algorithm with a lawyer.

Many technical experts in the AI field have criticized Lemoine's statements and questioned their scientific correctness. But his story has had the virtue of renewing a broad ethical debate that is certainly not over yet.

The Right Words in the Right Place

"I was surprised by the hype around this news. On the other hand, we are talking about an algorithm designed to do exactly that"—to sound like a person—says Enzo Pasquale Scilingo, a bioengineer at the Research Center E. Piaggio at the University of Pisa in Italy. Indeed, it is no longer a rarity to interact in a very normal way on the Web with users who are not actually human—just open the chat box on almost any large consumer Web site. "That said, I confess that reading the text exchanges between LaMDA and Lemoine made quite an impression on me!" Scilingo adds. Perhaps most striking are the exchanges related to the themes of existence and death, a dialogue so deep and articulate that it prompted Lemoine to question whether LaMDA could actually be sentient.

"First of all, it is essential to understand terminologies, because one of the great obstacles in scientific progress—and in neuroscience in particular—is the lack of precision of language, the failure to explain as exactly as possible what we mean by a certain word," says Giandomenico Iannetti, a professor of neuroscience at the Italian Institute of Technology and University College London. "What do we mean by 'sentient'? [Is it] the ability to register information from the external world through sensory mechanisms or the ability to have subjective experiences or the ability to be aware of being conscious, to be an individual different from the rest?"

"There is a lively debate about how to define consciousness," Iannetti continues. For some, it is being aware of having subjective experiences, what is called metacognition (Iannetti prefers the Latin term *metacognitione*), or thinking about thinking. The awareness of being conscious can disappear—for example, in people with dementia or in dreams—but this does not mean that the ability to have subjective experiences also disappears. "If we refer to the capacity that Lemoine ascribed to LaMDA—that is, the ability to become aware of its own existence ('become aware of its own existence' is a consciousness defined in the 'high sense,' or *metacognitione*), there is no 'metric' to say that an AI system has this property."

"At present," Iannetti says, "it is impossible to demonstrate this form of consciousness unequivocally even in humans." To estimate the state of consciousness in people, "we have only neurophysiological measures–for example, the complexity of brain activity in response to external stimuli." And these signs only allow researchers to infer the state of consciousness based on outside measurements.

Facts and Belief

About a decade ago engineers at Boston Dynamics began posting videos online of the first incredible tests of their robots. The footage showed technicians shoving or kicking the machines to demonstrate the robots' great ability to remain balanced. Many people were upset by this and called for a stop to it (and parody videos flourished). That emotional response fits in with the many, many experiments that have repeatedly shown the strength of the human tendency toward animism: attributing a soul to the objects around us, especially those we are most fond of or that have a minimal ability to interact with the world around them.

It is a phenomenon we experience all the time, from giving nicknames to automobiles to hurling curses at a malfunctioning computer. "The problem, in some way, is us," Scilingo says. "We attribute characteristics to machines that they do not and cannot have." He encounters this phenomenon with his and his colleagues' humanoid robot Abel, which is designed to emulate our facial expressions in order to convey emotions. "After seeing it in action," Scilingo says, "one of the questions I receive most often is 'But then does Abel feel emotions?' All these machines, Abel in this case, are designed to appear human, but I feel I can be peremptory in answering, 'No, absolutely not. As intelligent as they are, they cannot feel emotions. They are programmed to be believable.'"

"Even considering the theoretical possibility of making an AI system capable of simulating a conscious nervous system, a kind of in silico brain that would faithfully reproduce each element of the brain," two problems remain, Iannetti says. "The first is that, given the complexity of the system to be simulated, such a simulation is currently infeasible," he explains. "The second is that our brain inhabits a body that can move to explore the sensory environment necessary for consciousness and within which the organism that will become conscious develops. So the fact that LaMDA is a 'large language model' (LLM) means it generates sentences that can be plausible by *emulating* a nervous system but without attempting to *simulate* it. This precludes the possibility that it is conscious. Again, we see the importance of knowing the meaning of the terms we use–in this case, the difference between *simulation* and *emulation*."

In other words, having emotions is related to having a body. "If a machine claims to be afraid, and I believe it, that's my problem!" Scilingo says. "Unlike a human, a machine cannot, to date, have experienced the emotion of fear."

Beyond the Turing Test

But for bioethicist Maurizio Mori, president of the Italian Society for Ethics in Artificial Intelligence, these discussions are closely reminiscent of those that developed in the past about perception of pain in animals–or even infamous racist ideas about pain perception in humans.

"In past debates on self-awareness, it was concluded that the capacity for abstraction was a human prerogative, [with] Descartes denying that animals could feel pain because they lacked consciousness," Mori says. "Now, beyond this specific case raised by LaMDA–and which I do not have the technical tools to evaluate–I believe that the past has shown us that reality can often exceed imagination and that there is currently a widespread misconception about AI."

"There is indeed a tendency," Mori continues, "to 'appease'–explaining that machines are just machines–and an underestimation of the transformations that sooner or later may come with AI." He offers another example: "At the time of the first automobiles, it was reiterated at length that horses were irreplaceable."

Regardless of what LaMDA actually achieved, the issue of the difficult "measurability" of emulation capabilities expressed by machines also emerges. In the journal *Mind* in 1950, mathematician Alan Turing proposed a test to determine whether a machine was capable of exhibiting intelligent behavior, a game of imitation of some of the human cognitive functions. This type of test quickly became popular. It was reformulated and updated several times but continued to be something of an ultimate goal for many developers of intelligent machines. Theoretically, AIs capable of passing the test should be considered formally "intelligent" because they would be indistinguishable from a human being in test situations.

That may have been science fiction a few decades ago. Yet in recent years so many AIs have passed various versions of the Turing test that it is now a sort of relic of computer archaeology. "It makes less and less sense," Iannetti concludes, "because the development of emulation systems that reproduce more and more effectively what might be the output of a conscious nervous system makes the assessment of the plausibility of this output uninformative of the ability of the system that generated it to have subjective experiences."

One alternative, Scilingo suggests, might be to measure the "effects" a machine can induce on humans–that is, "how sentient that AI can be perceived to be by human beings."

A version of this article originally appeared in Le Scienze *and was reproduced with permission.*

About the Author

Leonardo De Cosmo is a freelance science journalist based in Rome. He loves exploring how science and technologies will shape the world.

Jellyfish, Sexbots and the Solipsism Problem

By John Horgan

What's the difference between science and philosophy? Scientists address questions that can in principle be answered by means of objective, empirical investigation. Philosophers wrestle with questions that cannot be empirically resolved and hence remain matters of taste, not truth.

Here is a classic philosophical question: What creatures and/or things are capable of consciousness? That is, who (and "who" is the right term, even if you're talking about a jellyfish or sexbot) belongs to the Consciousness Club?

This question animated "Animal Consciousness," a conference I attended at New York University last month. It should have been called "Animal Consciousness?" or "Animal 'Consciousness'" to reflect the uncertainty pervading the two-day meeting. Speakers disagreed over when and how consciousness evolved and what is required for it to occur. A nervous system? Brain? Complex responses to the environment? The ability to learn and adapt to new circumstances? And if we suspect that something is sentient, and hence capable of suffering, should we grant it rights?

In my last post, I focused on the debate over whether fish can suffer. Scholars also considered the sentience of dogs, lampreys, wasps, spiders, crustaceans and other species. Speakers presented evidence that creatures quite unlike us are capable of complex cognition.

Biologist Andrew Barron argued that bees, in spite of their minuscule brains, are not mindless automatons. Their capacity for learning rivals that of mammals. When harmed, bees stop eating and foraging as if they were depressed. Bees, Barron concludes, are conscious.

Does that mean all animals are? No, Barron doesn't think jellyfish, which lack a centralized nervous system, are conscious. If you poke a box jellyfish, it simply moves in the opposite direction. As Barron made the case for excluding jellyfish from the Consciousness Club, I felt sorry for them.

Philosopher Peter Singer, citing Barron's research on bees, considered whether cockroaches and bedbugs can suffer, and if so what, if anything, we should do about it. To convince us that octopuses are conscious, philosopher Peter Godfrey-Smith showed us a video of them goofing around while a pufferfish watched, seemingly out of pure curiosity.

Looming over these disputes is the solipsism problem. I know I am conscious, but I can't be absolutely sure that anything else is conscious, because I have access only to my own subjective experience. I'm pretty confident that you and other humans are conscious, because we're so similar. But my confidence in the consciousness of non-human things diminishes in proportion to their dissimilarity from me.

Neuroscientist Christof Koch suggested in his 2012 book *Consciousness* that someday science might solve the solipsism problem with a "consciousness meter." This hypothetical instrument could determine whether a jellyfish or smart phone is conscious and how conscious it is. Measuring an object's consciousness would be as straightforward as measuring its temperature.

The consciousness meter is a splendid example of begging the question. Scientists cannot build a consciousness meter until they reach agreement on what physical conditions are necessary and sufficient to produce consciousness. But scientists cannot reach agreement on those conditions unless they have a consciousness meter, a means of solving the solipsism problem.

As long as we lack a solution to the solipsism problem, theories of consciousness will be unconstrained and hence wildly divergent. Koch proselytizes for integrated information theory, which holds that even a single proton might be a little bit conscious. The theory implies that consciousness pervades the entire universe, as decreed by the ancient mystical doctrine panpsychism.

At the other extreme are so-called eliminative materialists, who question whether *anything* is really conscious, including humans. An advocate of this position is philosopher Daniel Dennett, who spoke at "Animal Consciousness." In his recent book *From Bacteria to Bach and Back*, Dennett calls consciousness an "illusion." He comes close to suggesting that we are zombies, beings that appear conscious but actually lack an inner life. (See my rebuttal of Dennett's argument here.)

The solipsism problem haunted other meetings at NYU I've attended over the past two years. At "Ethics of Artificial Intelligence," computer scientist Kate Devlin considered whether sexbots, robots designed to have sex with humans, might be conscious and hence deserving of rights. At a workshop on integrated information theory two years ago, Koch and other participants debated, only half jokingly, whether dark energy might conscious.

Last spring, NYU hosted "Is There Unconscious Perception?" Scholars argued over the implications of conditions such as blindsight, which is caused by brain damage. Subjectively, you feel blind, but if someone throws a ball at you, you will catch it. Blindsight proves that perception and other cognitive functions need not be accompanied by consciousness, according to philosopher Ned Block, an organizer of the meeting.

Block reiterated this point at "Animal Consciousness," which he also helped organize. Other scholars disagree with Block's interpretation of blindsight data, contending that people with blindsight might possess visual awareness even if they insist that they don't. That strikes me as a very weird claim. But my point is that even if you restrict your discussion of consciousness to humans, you can't escape the solipsism problem.

As long as we can't solve the solipsism problem, we will favor theories of consciousness for subjective reasons. You are big-hearted, so you grant consciousness to spiders, jellyfish, sexbots, dark energy and thermostats. (According to integrated information theory, it might feel like something to be a nuclear warhead!) I am a snooty tight-ass, so I restrict consciousness to humans, primates and a few especially clever birds, like crows. Your Consciousness Club is capacious, mine vanishingly small.

A wonderful, testy exchange between two grizzled philosophical warriors at "Animal Consciousness" exposed the profound divide in modern approaches to consciousness. On the stage was Dennett, who for decades has argued that conventional materialism can account for consciousness.

Sitting in the front row was Thomas Nagel, whose 1974 essay "What Is It Like to Be a Bat?" challenged materialist accounts of consciousness. Nagel reprised these arguments in his 2012 book *Mind and Cosmos: Why the Materialist Neo-Darwinian Conception of Nature Is Almost Certainly False*, which argues that science needs "a major conceptual revolution" to account for the emergence of life and consciousness.

Nagel asked Dennett "on what authority" he insists that consciousness can be reduced to brain states or some other conventional physical processes. Nagel seemed genuinely aggrieved. So did Dennett when he responded that explaining the world in physical terms is what science does. [See Clarification.] There is no rational reason to make an exception for consciousness.

Do you prefer Dennett's perspective, Nagel's, or something in between? You may think your preference is wholly rational and objective, but it is based more on taste than truth. We cannot escape our subjectivity when we try to solve the problem of subjectivity. Or so I argue in a book I am writing, *Mind-Body Problems*.

Clarification: Thomas Nagel, to whom I emailed this post, responded: "Your brief account of my exchange with Dennett leaves the issue somewhat obscure. My question was, by what authority does he allow his external view of himself as a physical system to overrule the evidence presented to him directly in his first-person experience. I think he acknowledges that this is a conflict over the authority of these two points of view in determining our conception of reality. He believes the first has decisive priority. I do not. But I certainly didn't feel 'aggrieved'– and neither, I'm sure, did Dan."

The views expressed are those of the author(s) and are not necessarily those of Scientific American.

About the Author

John Horgan directs the Center for Science Writings at the Stevens Institute of Technology. His books include The End of Science, The End of War and Mind-Body Problems*, available for free at mindbodyproblems.com. For many years he wrote the popular blog Cross Check for* Scientific American.

Section 4: Can Consciousness Be Explained by Science?

4.1 New Technique Seeks to Measure Consciousness
By Christof Koch

4.2 Will Science Ever Solve the Mysteries of Consciousness, Free Will and God?
By Michael Shermer

4.3 Computers Determine States of Consciousness
By Sam Rose

4.4 What God, Quantum Mechanics and Consciousness Have in Common
By John Horgan

4.5 *On Consciousness: Science and Subjectivity*: A Q&A with Bernard Baars
By Scott Barry Kaufman

4.6 Science Should Not Try to Absorb Religion and Other Ways of Knowing
By John Horgan

4.7 Free Will Is Only an Illusion if You Are, Too
By Alessandra Buccella and Tomáš Dominik

4.8 Where's My Consciousness-ometer?
By Tam Hunt

New Technique Seeks to Measure Consciousness

By Christof Koch

Measure what is measurable, and make measurable what is not so.

This quote from Galileo Galilei, one of the founding fathers of science, is a call to arms for ingenious bench scientists, clinicians and theoreticians to render consciousness measurable: to build an instrument that can tell whether that prone person who is nonresponsive or behaving in a reflexlike manner is actually conscious of something–of anything. Such a "consciousness meter" should reliably distinguish between a sleeper who is experiencing a vivid dream–even if she does not recall most of its content later on–and one who is in a dreamless, deep sleep, not feeling anything. Not just black but nothing, *nichts, nada, rien*. Or between a patient who is deeply anesthetized, and oblivious to the abdominal surgery being performed on him, and the rare cases of "awareness under anesthesia." Such a device should also be able to tell whether a grievously brain-injured patient, whose electroencephalograph (EEG) might be flat but who is moaning and occasionally moving his head or limbs, is experiencing pain or distress or is truly not conscious–alive but oblivious to the world.

Most scholars of consciousness aver that to be aware of something is to have a single, integrated experience. When looking at a sunset, for instance, you cannot separate the garish purple-orange hues from the bright globe about to sink below the horizon. Unless you are color-blind, color is a holistic aspect of your experience. When you are looking out at the world, you cannot make yourself be only conscious of the left or the right half of your visual field. You experience both. Whatever information you are conscious of is wholly and completely presented to your mind; it cannot be subdivided.

Underlying this unity of consciousness is a multitude of causal interactions among the relevant parts of the brain that create the mind. If areas of the brain start to disconnect or become fragmented and balkanized, as occurs in deep sleep or in anesthesia, consciousness fades and might cease altogether. Giulio Tononi, a neuroscientist, psychiatrist and expert on sleep and consciousness at the University of Wisconsin–Madison, has made this phenomenal aspect of consciousness the centerpiece of his Integrated Information Theory of consciousness.

Tononi, together with his colleague Marcello Massimini, now a professor at the University of Milan, Italy, and a few others set out to measure the extent to which the brain is integrated during sleep and during various pathological states.

The Bell of Consciousness

In a series of experiments, the researchers delivered a single, high-field pulse of magnetic energy via a technique called transcranial magnetic stimulation (TMS) to the heads of volunteers. Discharging a plastic-enclosed coil of wire held against the scalp induces a brief electric current in the gray matter underneath the skull (the subject feels a slight sting from stimulation of the skin). This pulse excites brain cells and nearby fibers of passage that will, in turn, engage synaptically connected neurons in a cascade of activity that reverberates inside the head. This electrical activity quickly dies out.

Tononi and Massimini rigged the subjects' scalp with 64 electrodes for recording the EEG while subjects were either quietly resting or asleep. When awake, the volunteers' EEG following the TMS pulse showed a typical waxing and waning pattern of fast, recurrent brain waves, lasting a third of a second or so. A mathematical analysis of the EEG signals revealed that a hotspot of high-amplitude potential traveled from the premotor cortex, above which the TMS coil was positioned, to the matching premotor cortex in the other hemisphere, to the motor cortex and to the posterior parietal cortices in the back. Think of the brain as a large church bell and the TMS device as the clapper. Once struck, a well-cast bell will ring at its characteristic pitch for a considerable time. And so does the awake cortex, buzzing between 10 to 40 times a second.

In contrast, the brain of a deep sleeper acts like a stunted, badly tuned bell. Whereas the initial amplitude of the EEG is larger than when a subject is awake, its duration is much shorter, and it does not reverberate across the cortex to other connected regions. Although the neurons remain active in sleep, as evidenced by the strong, local response, integration has broken down. Little of the spatially differentiated and temporally variegated sequence of electrical activity that is typical for the awake brain is present. The same is also true of subjects who volunteered to undergo general anesthesia with propofol or xenon. The TMS pulse invariably produces a simple response that remains local, indicative of a breakdown of cortico-cortical interactions and a lessening of integration.

Probing the Mind of a Patient

When severe injury strikes the brain, consciousness may not return. A car accident, a fall, a combat wound, a drug or alcohol overdose, a near drowning–any of these can lead to profound unconsciousness. Thanks to rescue helicopters and emergency medical technicians, who quickly deliver the victim to the care of a team of specialized trauma nurses and physicians, many patients can be plucked back from the edge of death. Although this is a blessing for most, it is a curse for a few. They remain alive for years, never recovering consciousness, undead.

Impaired states of consciousness include coma, the vegetative state and the minimally conscious state. Overall arousal fluctuates from complete absence in coma, to periodic sleep-wake transitions in the vegetative state, to conscious awakenings with purposeful movements in the minimally conscious state, to more or less continual awareness.

In the U.S. alone, as many as 25,000 patients hover for years in a persistent vegetative state. What makes the situation almost unbearable is that they can look and act as if they are fully present. Indeed, such patients have daily sleep-wake cycles. When they are "awake," their eyes are open and they may move reflexively; they may grimace, turn their head, groan. To the naive observer, these movements and sounds suggest that the patient is awake, trying to communicate with loved ones. The tragedy of the ruined patient's blank and empty life, drawn out over hopeless decades in hospices and nursing homes, is mirrored and amplified by the love–and the resources–her family expends on her care, always hoping for a miraculous recovery.

You may recall Terri Schiavo in Florida, who lingered for 15 years in a persistent vegetative state until her medically induced death in 2005. Because of the nasty, public fight between her husband, who advocated discontinuing life support, and her parents, who believed that their daughter had some measure of awareness, the case was litigated up and down the judicial chain, and eventually drew in then president George W. Bush. Medically, her case was uncontroversial. She had brief episodes of automatisms: head turning, eye movements and the like, but no reproducible or consistent, purposeful behavior. Her EEG was flat, indicating that her cerebral cortex had shut down. Her condition failed to improve over many years. The autopsy showed that her cortex had shrunk by half, with her visual centers atrophied; thus, contrary to public reports at the time, she could not have seen anything.

In contrast to Schiavo, minimally conscious patients have fluctuating signs of nonreflexive reactions, such as pursuing a target with their eyes or making verbal or hand responses to simple commands. Whereas consciousness has fled patients in a vegetative state, it is partially preserved in minimally conscious ones. It is, of course, absolutely critical to tell the difference between one and the other. Yet this is often not possible with purely behavioral-based measures.

Neurologist Steven Laureys of University Hospital in Liège, Belgium, Massimini, Tononi and their colleagues measured the span of brain integration in such patients. They applied TMS pulses to the parietal or frontal lobes of patients who had their eyes open. The result was unambiguous. Patients in a vegetative state had simple and local EEG responses—usually a slow, single positive-negative wave (when they had any response at all)—resembling the deep sleep and anesthesia response. Contrariwise, in minimally conscious patients, the magnetic pulse triggered the complex electrical responses expected of healthy, awake subjects. Five patients were additionally recruited from intensive care as soon as they awoke from coma. Three eventually recovered awareness, and two did not.

The onset of consciousness in those patients who did recover was preceded by a lengthening and complexification of the EEG response to the magnetic pulses—they progressed from a single localized wave to a much richer spatiotemporal pattern. In other words, this method can act as a crude consciousness meter. A miniaturized TMS coil in combination with an EEG device with a handful of electrodes can easily be assembled into an instrument.

In this way, theoretical insights into consciousness are married to clinical practice that benefits many.

Referenced

Breakdown of Cortical Effective Connectivity during Sleep. M. Massimini et al. in *Science*, Vol. 309, pages 2228–2232; September 30, 2005.

Recovery of Cortical Effective Connectivity and Recovery of Consciousness in Vegetative Patients. M. Rosanova et al. in *Brain*, Vol. 135, No. 4; pages 1308–1320; 2012.

About the Author

Christof Koch is chief scientific officer at the Allen institute for Brain Science in Seattle and Lois and Victor Troendle Professor of Cognitive and Behavioral Biology at the California Institute of Technology. He serves on Scientific American Mind's *board of advisers.*

Will Science Ever Solve the Mysteries of Consciousness, Free Will and God?

By Michael Shermer

In 1967 British biologist and Nobel laureate Sir Peter Medawar famously characterized science as, in book title form, *The Art of the Soluble*. "Good scientists study the most important problems they think they can solve. It is, after all, their professional business to solve problems, not merely to grapple with them," he wrote.

For millennia, the greatest minds of our species have grappled to gain purchase on the vertiginous ontological cliffs of three great mysteries—consciousness, free will and God—without ascending anywhere near the thin air of their peaks. Unlike other inscrutable problems, such as the structure of the atom, the molecular basis of replication and the causes of human violence, which have witnessed stunning advancements of enlightenment, these three seem to recede ever further away from understanding, even as we race ever faster to catch them in our scientific nets.

Are these "hard" problems, as philosopher David Chalmers characterized consciousness, or are they truly insoluble "mysterian" problems, as philosopher Owen Flanagan designated them (inspired by the 1960s rock group Question Mark and the Mysterians)? The "old mysterians" were dualists who believed in nonmaterial properties, such as the soul, that cannot be explained by natural processes. The "new mysterians," Flanagan says, contend that consciousness can never be explained because of the limitations of human cognition. I contend that not only consciousness but also free will and God are mysterian problems—not because we are not yet smart enough to solve them but because they can never be solved, not even in principle, relating to how the concepts are conceived in language. Call those of us in this camp the "final mysterians."

- **Consciousness.** The hard problem of consciousness is represented by the qualitative experiences (qualia) of what it is like to be something. It is the first-person subjective experience of the world through the senses and brain of the organism. It is not possible to know what it is like to be a bat (in philosopher Thomas Nagel's famous thought experiment), because if you altered your brain and body from humanoid to batoid, you would just be a bat, not a human knowing what it feels like to be a bat. You would not be like the traveling salesman in Franz Kafka's 1915 novella *The Metamorphosis*, who awakens to discover he has been transformed into a giant insect but still has human thoughts. You would just be an arthropod. By definition, only I can know my first-person experience of being me, and the same is true for you, bats and bugs.

- **Free will.** Few scientists dispute that we live in a deterministic universe in which all effects have causes (except in quantum mechanics, although this just adds an element of randomness to the system, not freedom). And yet we all act as if we have free will—that we make choices among options and retain certain degrees of freedom within constraining systems. Either we are all delusional, or else the problem is framed to be conceptually impenetrable. We are not inert blobs of matter bandied about the pinball machine of life by the paddles of nature's laws; we are active agents within the causal net of the universe, both determined by it and helping to determine it through our choices. That is the compatibilist position from whence volition and culpability emerge.
- **God.** If the creator of the universe is supernatural—outside of space and time and nature's laws—then by definition, no natural science can discover God through any measurements made by natural instruments. By definition, this God is an unsolvable mystery. If God is part of the natural world or somehow reaches into our universe from outside of it to stir the particles (to, say, perform miracles like healing the sick), we should be able to quantify such providential acts. This God is scientifically soluble, but so far all claims of such measurements have yet to exceed statistical chance. In any case, God as a natural being

who is just a whole lot smarter and more powerful than us is not what most people conceive of as deific.

Although these final mysteries may not be solvable by science, they are compelling concepts nonetheless, well deserving of our scrutiny if for no other reason than it may lead to a deeper understanding of our nature as sentient, volitional, spiritual beings.

About the Author

Michael Shermer is publisher of Skeptic *magazine (www.skeptic.com) and a Presidential Fellow at Chapman University. His new book is* Heavens on Earth: The Scientific Search for the Afterlife, Immortality, and Utopia *(Henry Holt, 2018).*

Computers Determine States of Consciousness

By Sam Rose

Consciousness is a peculiar, even supernatural idea. From three pounds of flesh emerges an awareness of the body that houses it and the world around it. We all recognize consciousness when we see it, but what is it, really? And where does it go when it's gone? Neuroscience doesn't have the tools to answer these questions–if they're really possible to answer at all–but in a hospital, doctors need to be able to diagnose consciousness. They need to know if a patient with a brain injury is aware of himself or surroundings. This diagnosis is still mostly made with a simple bedside exam. Is the patient following commands? Is he gesturing or verbalizing purposefully, etc.?

For patients at the edge of consciousness–not lucid but not comatose either–defining the state of consciousness is difficult. Purposeless movements and sounds can look a lot like purposeful ones. Awareness comes and goes. In many, a high stakes diagnosis will be made. The patient is either in a minimally conscious state, where there's some likelihood of recovery, or the patient is given a diagnosis of unresponsive wakefulness syndrome, where the actions are deemed random and purposeless and there's little hope of recovery. Troublingly, these diagnoses are mixed up in as many as 40% of cases.

With a great deal at stake, a recent study in the journal *Brain* tries to give doctors a little help. The article details a machine learning algorithm that distinguishes unresponsive wakefulness syndrome from a minimally conscious state using EEG brainwave recordings. The algorithm, if put into use, would take some of the guesswork out of this diagnosis, and likely perform better than most human doctors. But diagnosing state-of-mind with an algorithm raises ethical concerns. How comfortable are we with turning over this kind of life-or-death diagnosis to a machine, especially since our handle on consciousness, as an idea, is so minimal?

Looking into the brain for traces of consciousness is not a new idea. For decades, researchers have been studying how brain scanning techniques like PET and fMRI could be used to study the edge of consciousness. In a landmark 2014 study, PET scans showed that brains could respond to cues in some patients given a (mis)diagnosis of unresponsive wakefulness syndrome. What's more is that the patients with an active PET scan were more likely to make a meaningful recovery.

This finding argues that PET scans should be used if there's any doubt about a patient's state of consciousness. PET scans, though, aren't available in every hospital. They're also expensive, prone to artifact, and difficult to interpret. A more accessible alternative is electroencephalography or EEG, where electrical sensors are placed on the patient's scalp, picking up activity through the skull. EEG registers brain activity as waves when enough neurons fire in unison. In a healthy person, these waves undulate at predictable frequencies. After a brain injury, the pattern is less predictable.

In the new study, a group at Pitié-Salpêtrière Hospital in Paris took EEG recordings from 268 patients diagnosed with either unresponsive wakefulness syndrome or a minimally conscious state. The EEGs were recorded before and during a listening task designed to pick up on the conscious processing of sounds. Dozens of aspects of the data were fed into a machine learning algorithm called a DOC-Forest.

The DOC-Forest performed relatively well at this complex task. Roughly 3 out of 4 cases were diagnosed properly. (Note: instead of accuracy, the authors use a better performance metric called AUC. AUC takes into account the rate of false positive classification, which has profound consequences here.)

The authors also took care to push the DOC-Forest into real world scenarios. They introduced random noise into the data, simulating what differences in data collection procedures might look like. They took into account different arrangements of sensors on the skull.

They also used the algorithm on a different set of patients from a hospital in Liege, Belgium. In each case, the DOC-Forest performed well, with roughly the same performance measure.

From a certain perspective, this machine learning algorithm is a significant advance. EEG data is complex and contains multiple dimensions–time, frequency, testing condition, sensor locations, etc. Think pages and pages of squiggly waves on a computer screen. Typically, researchers would focus on a handful of easy-to-interpret aspects of the data, say the appearance of a specific brainwave during the listening task. This focus on interpretation excludes potentially important aspects of the data, though. Machine learning doesn't have this human bias toward interpretability and communicability. It just focuses on classifying the data correctly, which is all that's needed here.

If put into practice, the DOC-Forest could be a helpful tool for an inexperienced neurologist. The DOC-Forest would run through the squiggly lines of EEG data and provide odds that the patient has some level of consciousness that the inexperienced doctor missed in his or her bedside tests. There's a circularity here, though. The algorithm is "trained" on cases that human neurologists diagnosed with bedside tests. While the group at Pitié-Salpêtrière was able to track patients for some time to minimize misdiagnoses, the algorithm just associates EEG signals with those–albeit more expert–bedside diagnoses. What, though, of a form of consciousness that's not revealed in any of these tests, EEG or otherwise? Keep in mind we don't really know where and how consciousness emerges. We don't have much sense of the forms conscious experience may take outside of the ones we experience for ourselves. One could argue our minimal understanding of the problem means that we shouldn't get the machines involved quite yet. On the other hand, it's not clear that we'll ever have satisfying answers to these questions. So, why not let a carefully designed tool, like the DOC-Forest, help make decisions within our current understanding of consciousness. There's no easy answer, but it's something that should probably be discussed as these tools push closer to everyday use.

About the Author

Sam Rose is a postdoctoral scholar at Duke University. He researches pharmacological approaches for treating brain diseases. You can reach him by email at samueljosephrose@gmail.com.

What God, Quantum Mechanics and Consciousness Have in Common

By John Horgan

In my 20s, I had a friend who was brilliant, charming, Ivy-educated and rich, heir to a family fortune. I'll call him Gallagher. He could do anything he wanted. He experimented, dabbling in neuroscience, law, philosophy and other fields. But he was so critical, so *picky*, that he never settled on a career. Nothing was good enough for him. He never found love for the same reason. He also disparaged his friends' choices, so much so that he alienated us. He ended up bitter and alone. At least that's my guess. I haven't spoken to Gallagher in decades.

There is such a thing as being too picky, especially when it comes to things like work, love and nourishment (even the pickiest eater has to eat *something*). That's the lesson I gleaned from Gallagher. But when it comes to answers to big mysteries, most of us aren't picky enough. We settle on answers for bad reasons, for example, because our parents, priests or professors believe it. We think we need to believe *something*, but actually we don't. We can, and should, decide that no answers are good enough. We should be agnostics.

Some people confuse agnosticism (not knowing) with apathy (not caring). Take Francis Collins, a geneticist who directs the National Institutes of Health. He is a devout Christian, who believes that Jesus performed miracles, died for our sins and rose from the dead. In his 2006 bestseller *The Language of God*, Collins calls agnosticism a "cop-out." When I interviewed him, I told him I am an agnostic and objected to "cop-out."

Collins apologized. "That was a put-down that should not apply to earnest agnostics who have considered the evidence and still don't find an answer," he said. "I was reacting to the agnosticism I see in the scientific community, which has not been arrived at by a careful examination of the evidence." I have examined the evidence for Christianity, and I find it unconvincing. I'm not convinced by any scientific creation stories, either, such as those that depict our cosmos as a bubble in an oceanic "multiverse."

People I admire fault me for being too skeptical. One is the late religious philosopher Huston Smith, who called me "convictionally impaired." Another is megapundit Robert Wright, an old friend, with whom I've often argued about evolutionary psychology and Buddhism. Wright once asked me in exasperation, "Don't you believe *anything*?" Actually, I believe lots of things, for example, that war is bad and should be abolished.

But when it comes to theories about ultimate reality, I'm with Voltaire. "Doubt is not a pleasant condition," Voltaire said, "but certainty is an absurd one." Doubt protects us from dogmatism, which can easily morph into fanaticism and what William James calls a "premature closing of our accounts with reality." Below I defend agnosticism as a stance toward the existence of God, interpretations of quantum mechanics and theories of consciousness. When considering alleged answers to these three riddles, we should be as picky as my old friend Gallagher.

The Problem of Evil

Why do we exist? The answer, according to the major monotheistic religions, including the Catholic faith in which I was raised, is that an all-powerful, supernatural entity created us. This deity loves us, as a human father loves his children, and wants us to behave in a certain way. If we're good, He'll reward us. If we're bad, He'll punish us. (I use the pronoun "He" because most scriptures describe God as male.)

My main objection to this explanation of reality is the problem of evil. A casual glance at human history, and at the world today, reveals enormous suffering and injustice. If God loves us and is omnipotent, why is life so horrific for so many people? A standard response to this question is that God gave us free will; we can choose to be bad as well as good.

The late, great physicist Steven Weinberg, an atheist, who died in July, slaps down the free will argument in his book *Dreams of a Final Theory*. Noting that Nazis killed many of his relatives in the Holocaust, Weinberg asks: Did millions of Jews have to die so the Nazis could exercise their free will? That doesn't seem fair. And what about kids who get cancer? Are we supposed to think that cancer cells have free will?

On the other hand, life isn't always hellish. We experience love, friendship, adventure and heartbreaking beauty. Could all this really come from random collisions of particles? Even Weinberg concedes that life sometimes seems "more beautiful than strictly necessary." If the problem of evil prevents me from believing in a loving God, then the problem of beauty keeps me from being an atheist like Weinberg. Hence, agnosticism.

The Problem of Information

Quantum mechanics is science's most precise, powerful theory of reality. It has predicted countless experiments, spawned countless applications. The trouble is, physicists and philosophers disagree over what it means, that is, what it says about how the world works. Many physicists–most, probably–adhere to the Copenhagen interpretation, advanced by Danish physicist Niels Bohr. But that is a kind of anti-interpretation, which says physicists should not try to make sense of quantum mechanics; they should "shut up and calculate," as physicist David Mermin once put it.

Philosopher Tim Maudlin deplores this situation. In his 2019 book *Philosophy of Physics: Quantum Theory*, he points out that several interpretations of quantum mechanics describe in detail how the world works. These include the GRW model proposed by Ghirardi, Rimini and Weber; the pilot-wave theory of David Bohm; and the many-worlds hypothesis of Hugh Everett. But here's the irony: Maudlin is so scrupulous in pointing out the flaws of these interpretations that he reinforces my skepticism. They all seem hopelessly kludgy and preposterous.

Maudlin does not examine interpretations that recast quantum mechanics as a theory about information. For positive perspectives on information-based interpretations, check out *Beyond Weird* by journalist Philip Ball and *The Ascent of Information* by astrobiologist Caleb Scharf. But to my mind, information-based takes on quantum mechanics are even less plausible than the interpretations that Maudlin scrutinizes. The concept of information makes no sense without conscious beings to send, receive and act upon the information.

Introducing consciousness into physics undermines its claim to objectivity. Moreover, as far as we know, consciousness arises only in certain organisms that have existed for a brief period here on Earth. So how can quantum mechanics, if it's a theory of information rather than matter and energy, apply to the entire cosmos since the big bang? Information-based theories of physics seem like a throwback to geocentrism, which assumed the universe revolves around us. Given the problems with all interpretations of quantum mechanics, agnosticism, again, strikes me as a sensible stance.

Mind-Body Problems

The debate over consciousness is even more fractious than the debate over quantum mechanics. How does matter make a mind? A few decades ago, a consensus seemed to be emerging. Philosopher Daniel Dennett, in his cockily titled *Consciousness Explained*, asserted that consciousness clearly emerges from neural processes, such as electrochemical pulses in the brain. Francis Crick and Christof Koch proposed that consciousness is generated by networks of neurons oscillating in synchrony.

Gradually, this consensus collapsed, as empirical evidence for neural theories of consciousness failed to materialize. As I point out in my recent book *Mind-Body Problems*, there are now a dizzying variety of theories of consciousness. Christof Koch has thrown his weight behind integrated information theory, which holds that consciousness might be a property of all matter, not just brains.

This theory suffers from the same problems as information-based theories of quantum mechanics. Theorists such as Roger Penrose, who won last year's Nobel Prize in Physics, have conjectured that quantum effects underpin consciousness, but this theory is even more lacking in evidence than integrated information theory.

Researchers cannot even agree on what form a theory of consciousness should take. Should it be a philosophical treatise? A purely mathematical model? A gigantic algorithm, perhaps based on Bayesian computation? Should it borrow concepts from Buddhism, such as anatta, the doctrine of no self? All of the above? None of the above? Consensus seems farther away than ever. And that's a good thing. We should be open-minded about our minds.

So, what's the difference, if any, between me and Gallagher, my former friend? I like to think it's a matter of style. Gallagher scorned the choices of others. He resembled one of those mean-spirited atheists who revile the faithful for their beliefs. I try not to be dogmatic in my disbelief, and to be sympathetic toward those who, like Francis Collins, have found answers that work for them. Also, I get a kick out of inventive theories of everything, such as John Wheeler's "it from bit" and Freeman Dyson's principle of maximum diversity, even if I can't embrace them.

I'm definitely a skeptic. I doubt we'll ever know whether God exists, what quantum mechanics means, how matter makes mind. These three puzzles, I suspect, are different aspects of a single, impenetrable mystery at the heart of things. But one of the pleasures of agnosticism—perhaps the greatest pleasure—is that I can keep looking for answers and hoping that a revelation awaits just over the horizon.

This is an opinion and analysis article; the views expressed by the author or authors are not necessarily those of Scientific American.

About the Author

John Horgan directs the Center for Science Writings at the Stevens Institute of Technology. His books include The End of Science, The End of War *and* Mind-Body Problems, *available for free at mindbodyproblems.com. For many years he wrote the popular blog Cross Check for* Scientific American.

On Consciousness: Science and Subjectivity: A Q&A with Bernard Baars

By Scott Barry Kaufman

Far from being some free-floating cloud around our heads, sensory consciousness is profoundly embedded in biology, anatomy, physiology, and above all, in adaptive functions that serve us in every waking second of life. This is not some philosophical speculation. It is now supported by numerous findings published in peer-reviewed journals that are easily found in web archives.

One of my favorite thinkers and researchers on this topic is Bernard Baars. Baars fundamentally changed the scientific study of consciousness over 30 years ago and he has done it again in a stimulating update on consciousness called *On Consciousness: Science & Subjectivity–Updated Works on Global Workspace Theory*. In his new book he proposes novel predictions and draws on the latest research in cognitive science. This magnum opus is really incredible and should be on the bookshelf for anyone seriously interested in wrestling with the paradoxes and mysteries of human consciousness. In this interview with Baars, we discuss his new book and his latest thoughts on the scientific study of consciousness.

Q: How did you get interested in the scientific study of consciousness?

A: I couldn't avoid it. I was interested in philosophy, where every major voice had something to say about consciousness. Then I read A.J. Ayer, a famous logical positivist, who made the case that English and American philosophy since Bertrand Russell was essentially a non-empirical enterprise. I was a newbie, so maybe I got that totally wrong, but I became a psychology major and lucked out. My brilliant introductory professor had us read George A. Miller's beautiful little history book, *Psychology: The science of mental life*.

That did it for me, because under the professional strictures of behaviorism you were not supposed to talk about "mental life," and Miller made the case (in a very polite way) that the radical behaviorists were wrong. I had no idea at that time that the Harvard Psychology Department had actually split in two in the 1950s over that debate. The half called "psychology" was known for B.F. Skinner's radical behaviorism, and the new Social Relations department had the most famous sensory psychologist of the time, S.S. (Smitty) Stevens. A very famous article by C.P. Snow, a British scientist-novelist, had publicized what was called the "split culture" pitting the sciences against the traditional humanities. Historians still view that as a disaster.

So I had fabulous professors who were sincere and eager to communicate, and who privately wondered about the same things. Almost everything I've written since then had its beginnings in the research programs of my undergrad and grad professors. Even B.F. Skinner changed his mind about radical behaviorism in his two-volume autobiography in 1976, called *Particulars of my Life*. That's a Shakespeare quote, and it came from his four-year undergraduate quest to become a stream of consciousness novelist.

I'm interested in all aspects of human nature. When I started in 1980 as a cognitive scientist, behaviorism was still powerful and nobody wanted to study consciousness directly. It was considered to be career suicide. Cognitive science in the 80s was a much more broad-minded approach to psychology than the others at the time–where we incorporated artificial intelligence, linguistics, anthropology, neural networks, and language science–I enjoyed it immensely.

When you ask how I wandered into the lone forest of consciousness and the brain, which is now a coherent field of science, I have to blame the whole history of Western ideas going back to classical Greece. But that even looks arbitrary these days. Now that we have another thousand years of ancient history it's obvious that the Indus Valley Civilization had a flourishing trade with Sumer, which was part of the Fertile Crescent, where people carried on constant trade and had early cuneiform alphabets, enormous archives of them. On top of that, the Greco-Buddhist Empire of Ashoka imported Greek sculptors, and the Indo-European languages were already spoken across most of the Eurasian landmass. So the whole idea of East is East and West is West and never the twain shall meet is an intentional joke, because Rudyard Kipling knew all about the Greco-Buddhist Empire.

In every wisdom tradition I know, subjectivity (aka consciousness) is a central topic, perhaps because it combines the individual with the social group in such an obvious way. Our individuality is a function of the cortex, which is now proven by brain studies to be "the organ of consciousness." Wilder Penfield discovered that in 1934 via open-brain surgeries in fully awake patients, who were able to talk with him and gesture. Over three decades he studied about 1,200 patients at the Montreal Neurological Institute. That surgery is still being done, and the biomedical archives are full of direct evidence. Just do a search on "conscious" AND "brain" and it pops up.

Anyway, as you know, consciousness had been neglected for about 100 years since William James. This was an enormous opportunity and challenge, of course, and I could see ways of scientifically addressing it.

Scientific work may look humdrum to outsiders, but many scientists experience it as a kind of creative struggle, filled with practical and conceptual challenges that have never before been solved. We only need to look at the growth in genomics today for endless examples. But what can the creative aspect of science tell us about our mindbrain? This term 'mindbrain science' comes from neuroscientist Jakk Panksepp's wonderful books on emotion, and I think he wanted to emphasize that mind and brain are not separate, they are profoundly linked.

So, in 1982, I was able to combine the idea of a global workspace architecture with the stream of consciousness. In a way, it combined the novel idea of "swarm computing" with the evidence we had about the limited capacity of the conscious stream. The empirical theory was called Global Workspace Theory, or GWT.

GWT continues to grow with more and more evidence. The idea has since entered mainstream science.

Consciousness is a fundamental concept, like mass and energy, entropy and life. Scientists can't avoid it, so we use any number of pseudonyms. People call it "perception" or "attention" or even "knowledge." Those terms capture part of the truth, but they are by no means the whole network of empirically anchored concepts.

The empirical anchors of conscious events are emerging even today, with some real progress on cortical markers for conscious events that are comparable to experimentally matched unconscious ones. This is an emerging field, but it is being developed in a very reliable way by excellent researchers.

Q: What is Global Workspace Theory?

A: Global Workspace Theory is an effort to understand the biggest empirical paradox that I know of in the very broad field of psychobiology (stretching from consciousness all the way to deep biology). I call this well-known puzzle a "paradox," because I don't know the answer. But GWT is an effort to make some sense out of it.

Global Workspace Theory came out of the realization by people like Alan Newell, Herbert A. Simon, Donald Norman, and Daniel Kahneman that the narrowness of the stream of consciousness seemed to conflict with the enormous capacity of unconscious "memories," or "automatisms," or whatever people called them. You have this fabulous "memory" domain that no one has any quantitative estimate of, and it's all run by this "tiny rivulet," as William James called it. He couldn't figure it out either, but he knew the evidence.

Alan Newell's group at Carnegie-Mellon University had the insight that none of the available algorithms could solve the ARPA challenge of identifying 1,000 spoken words. So they found a kind of swarm-computational answer: If you put a hundred crummy algorithms together and let them share hypotheses and vote on the most popular one, it turns out that very inadequate algorithms could jointly solve problems that no single one could solve.

People had been thinking about parallel computers, and parallel-interactive problem solving, and a small group of neural network pioneers somehow arrived at a very similar view, perhaps from considering the many layered arrays in the brain.

That turned into Global Workspace Theory as a way to organize a lot of evidence about closely similar conscious and unconscious brain processing. We studied dichotic listening, where the subject wore headphones with two input channels, left and right, and had to say the heard syllables as fast as possible. It was called "shadowing" the input. People can do that extremely well, the only cost being the fact that the "Unattended" ear is totally unconscious. But I read a beautiful experiment by Donald G. MacKay, who discovered that an ambiguous word in the conscious (attended) channel could be changed by an unconscious word at the same moment in the "unconscious" channel. The phenomenon of unconscious brain events shaping conscious ones is now routinely studied, although it is still described in behavioristic terms.

Now we have fabulous brain instruments and we can actually observe signal processing in vision and hearing, not with "ground truth" precision, but good enough to test hypotheses. I had the good fortune to work with Gerald Edelman on these questions, and by now it's very clear that the cortex is the perfect brain structure for a "dynamic" global workspace.

My current research extends the Global Workspace (GW) theory of conscious experience to brain evidence, particularly the role of the cortex and thalamus. While cortex and thalamus look separate to the naked eye, they act as an integrated system (Llinas and Pare, 1991; Edelman and Tononi, 2000; Steriade, 2006; Freeman, 2007).

Conscious state studies typically compare waking to slow-wave sleep, coma, general anesthesia, and the epilepsies. Studies of conscious contents compare conscious vs. unconscious cognition during the waking state, using binocular rivalry, the attentional blink, backward masking, and attentional manipulations. Both conscious and unconscious stimuli trigger sensory volleys that can be traced well into the cortex (Gaillard et al., 2009; Panagiotaropoulos et al., 2012).

Brain imaging experiments have supported the best-known GW prediction of "widespread integration and broadcasting" (Dehaene and Naccache, 2001). That is, conscious stimuli typically evoke cortical activity that is more widespread, intense, and correlated than matched unconscious stimuli.

Part IV of my latest book *On Consciousness: Science & Subjectivity* develops GW dynamics, suggesting that conscious experiences reflect a flexible "binding and broadcasting" function in the brain, which is able to mobilize a large, distributed collection of specialized cortical networks and processes that are not conscious by themselves. Note that the "broadcast" phase proposed by the theory should evoke widespread adaptation, for the same reason that a fire alarm should evoke widespread responding, because the specific needs for task-relevant responders cannot be completely known ahead of time. General alarms are interpreted according to local conditions.

A brain-based GW interacts with an "audience" of highly distributed, specialized knowledge sources, which interpret the global signal in terms of local knowledge (Baars, 1988). The global signal triggers reentrant signaling, resonance is the typical activity of the cortex.

Q. What is the proposed biological function of consciousness?

A: A great body of evidence suggests that conscious sensation and cognition provides the leading edge of moment-to-moment adaptation to the sensory, social, and conceptual world. Darwinian evolution occurs over generations, and by epigenetic expression it also regulates life development. But animals encounter very fast changes in the world, which are novel and ambiguous. To adapt to fast and ill-defined dangers and opportunities we need the brain.

Cortical sensory consciousness is believed to operate around 10 Hz, which is the theta and alpha range of brain oscillations. If you're a rabbit confronted with a potential snake, you first have to run to safety, and then try to evaluate what you saw. The 100 ms domain (10 Hz) is a very useful dwell time for sensory input, and it's also the sniffing rate of small, ancestral mammals. Biologically the 100 ms domain makes a great deal of sense, and consciousness is clearly biological. It has to have plausible bio-functions.

New evidence now also implicated the slower delta range. It is possible that these slow oscillations are modulated by beta and gamma oscillations that carry content, along with spatial arrays that are linked point-to-point by "labeled line" connections. This is a very exciting frontier.

Q: What does Global Workspace Theory predict about conscious cognition?

A: Like any other theory, it has numerous implications. I address just this question in my newest book, *On Consciousness: Science & Subjectivity - Updated Works on Global Workspace Theory* (The Nautilus Press, 2019), laying out a framework for the role of conscious and unconscious experiences in the living brain.

The most novel prediction of GWT is the idea of a global broadcast linked to conscious – but not unconscious – events in the brain. It has received substantial corroboration from several laboratories.

Q: How does modern science go about studying consciousness?

A: Consciousness is a part of nature, and we now have clear evidence about the "organ of the conscious mind," the cerebral cortex, which fills 80 percent of the cranial volume. Broadly, sensory perception is conscious, while "stored memory traces" are not. Endogenous senses like inner speech and visual imagery are also conscious, perhaps more vividly in children.

The most revealing studies compare matched conscious and unconscious conditions, aka "contrastive analysis," and that has allowed us to pinpoint the location and processes that give rise to visual consciousness, for instance.

Q: Has there been scientific progress?

A: Yes, an enormous amount. When I first proposed GWT in 1982 all we had was psychological evidence and a new understanding of "parallel-interactive processing." Both were vital. But now we can look directly at the living brain at high spatio-temporal resolution, we can trace the fiber system, and we can see how cortex is wired to allow "global integration and broadcasting."

We also understand why the cortex is so enormously flexible, and we have new experimental tools.

Cortex can be traced via the fossil record to come even before the mammals. The current weight of evidence suggests that all "cortical" animals are at least sensorily conscious. Humans have the added advantage of spoken language and more precise use of meanings, which depend on the association areas of cortex. There are alternative proposals for the biological basis of consciousness, but they don't have the enormous bandwidth of cortex.

As you know, there are some simple and informative ways to study the stream of consciousness (SoC). The subjective world is not inaccessible. People can tell us an enormous amount about their conscious inner lives. You can study spontaneous fantasy, creativity, and post-traumatic intrusions. The cortex is essentially never "at rest" as long as it is awake, so the term "resting state" is misleading. The conscious component of cortex is always active, even in dreams, and it is simply part of the causal network of nature. It's not something that lives in some other metaphysical space.

Now that we have amazingly good brain instruments, we can also study sensory processes at the level of neurons. What is new, I believe, is what I've called "contrastive analysis," which is the precise experimental comparison between closely matched conscious and unconscious events. It allows us "to treat consciousness as an empirical variable." And then we test hypotheses that are falsifiable, in a Karl Popper fashion.

This has been worked out very beautifully in two ways: sensory competition (like binocular rivalry), and what is called the Attentional Blink (AB). Both methods allow close experimental comparisons between nearly-identical conscious and unconscious threads in the brain. The conscious ones we know, because we can describe them; and the matched unconscious conditions are not reportable, but they can be studied via direct cortical recording. Now we can ask, What makes conscious brain activities different from all the others? And there we get a growing family of global workspace (GW) theories.

In science the trick is to pinpoint the empirically answerable questions. Around 1900 physics realized that the "cosmic ether" was not testable, so they dropped it. In biology they dropped the "life force" of Henri Bergson, because it was not testable. Even Einstein gave up on trying to understand quantum phenomena in classical terms. Empirical testability allows us to sweep away speculations, and this simplifies things immensely.

I'm particularly fond of work done at the CNRS in Paris by Stanislas Dehaene and Jean-Pierre Changeux, first-rate scientists, and by the Max Planck research group in Tuebingen, Germany, led by Nikos Logothetis and Fanis Panagiotaropoulos et al. (2012) building on almost two decades of findings from intracranial recordings in the macaque. They used an experimental technique called "flash suppression," involving a long-lasting type of binocular rivalry between the conscious (perceived) and matched unconscious (unperceived) sensory input. This method allows for "contrastive analysis" of conscious vs. unconscious contents with identical stimulus presentation to the two eyes.

I'm glad that this work broadly confirms a prediction I made in 1982, the "global workspace" hypothesis, which is kind of an "integration and broadcasting" function in the visual brain, exactly where you would expect it: in areas IT/MTL where visual input is integrated into coherent Gestalts.

IT/MTL is where we organize visual information into "people, buildings, and scenes." So it is an area of high-level integration and broadcasting of visual information. The "broadcast" or "ignition" appears to be propagated to other parts of cortex.

The area called MTL is the hippocampus, which now appears to be the first experiential "holding buffer" for memories that will later be spread to cortex and other regions. It takes the traces of moment-to-moment experiences and turns them into vast numbers of synaptic connections. The conscious cortex is the leading edge of moment-to-moment adaptation to new and significant events in the world. It is not some floating halo around the head.

Q: What about the "Hard Problem" of mind versus the physical world?

A: With apologies to my friend David Chalmers, the "Hard Problem" has no supportive evidence. Neither does the new proposal of panpsychism, which is not falsifiable as it is described. Science can only use empirically testable hypotheses.

The "mind-body" question, in various guises, is ancient, but it is posed as an all-or-none dichotomy, as if mind must be the basis of brain, or vice versa. This is like asking which came first, the chicken or the egg? You divide the world into two halves and expect a sensible answer. It doesn't work. What you need is to study the genome and its phenotypical expressions; this is very complex and the answer is never "one causes the other." It's always a set of interactions. The Hard Problem tries to shoehorn all that into simple categories and it's not testable.

I make a rule of ignoring any ideas that are untestable empirically, and of focusing on the testable ones. A very old practice in the history of science, which allows us to filter out empty scholasticism – following Karl Popper's rule that empirical hypotheses have to be falsifiable, or they are useless. This was crucial to physics and biology in the 20th century.

It seems to be very difficult for people to think of consciousness as a natural phenomenon. But now we have decades of evidence and some theory that points to that idea.

Q: How are you pursuing these ideas today?

A: There's a huge task of communicating the new science. My editor Natalie Geld and I are constantly working together to reach out to educated audiences, via our latest book, *On Consciousness: Science & Subjectivity*, talks, virtual seminars, and our new podcast *On Consciousness* with my co-host, neuroscientist David Edelman. I'm exploring other cortical hypotheses and answering some new questions with mathematicians.

The views expressed are those of the author(s) and are not necessarily those of Scientific American.

About the Author

Scott Barry Kaufman, Ph.D., is a humanistic psychologist exploring the depths of human potential. He has taught courses on intelligence, creativity, and well-being at Columbia University, NYU, the University of Pennsylvania, and elsewhere. He hosts The Psychology Podcast, and is author and/or editor of 9 books, including Transcend: The New Science of Self-Actualization, Wired to Create: Unravelling the Mysteries of the Creative Mind *(with Carolyn Gregoire), and* Ungifted: Intelligence Redefined. *In 2015, he was named one of "50 Groundbreaking Scientists who are changing the way we see the world" by* Business Insider. *Find out more at http://ScottBarryKaufman.com. He wrote the extremely popular Beautiful Minds blog for* Scientific American *for close to a decade.*

Science Should Not Try to Absorb Religion and Other Ways of Knowing

By John Horgan

An edgy biography of Stephen Hawking has me reminiscing about science's good old days. Or were they bad? I can't decide. I'm talking about the 1990s, when scientific hubris ran rampant. As journalist Charles Seife recalls in *Hawking Hawking: The Selling of a Scientific Celebrity*, Hawking and other physicists convinced us that they were on the verge of a "theory of everything" that would solve the riddle of existence. It would reveal why there is something rather than nothing, and why that something is the way it is.

In this column, I'll look at an equally ambitious and closely related claim, that science will absorb other ways of seeing the world, including the arts, humanities and religion. Nonscientific modes of knowledge won't necessarily vanish, but they will become consistent with science, our supreme source of truth. The most eloquent advocate of this perspective is biologist Edward Wilson, one of our greatest scientist-writers.

In his 1998 bestseller *Consilience: The Unity of Knowledge*, Wilson prophesies that science will soon yield such a compelling, complete theory of nature, including human nature, that "the humanities, ranging from philosophy and history to moral reasoning, comparative religion, and interpretation of the arts, will draw closer to the sciences and partly fuse with them." Wilson calls this unification of knowledge "consilience," an old-fashioned term for coming together or converging. Consilience will resolve our age-old identity crisis, helping us understand once and for all "who we are and why we are here," as Wilson puts it.

Dismissing philosophers' warnings against deriving "ought" from "is," Wilson insists that we can deduce moral principles from science. Science can illuminate our moral impulses and emotions, such as our love for those who share our genes, as well as giving us moral guidance. This linkage of science to ethics is crucial, because Wilson wants us to share his desire to preserve nature in all its wild variety, a goal that he views as an ethical imperative.

At first glance you might wonder: Who could possibly object to this vision? Wouldn't we all love to agree on a comprehensive worldview, consistent with science, that tells us how to behave individually and collectively? And in fact. many scholars share Wilson's hope for a merger of science with alternative ways of engaging with reality. Some enthusiasts have formed the Consilience Project, dedicated to "developing a body of social theory and analysis that explains and seeks solutions to the unique challenges we face today." Last year, poet-novelist Clint Margrave wrote an eloquent defense of consilience for *Quillette,* noting that he has "often drawn inspiration from science."

Another consilience booster is psychologist and megapundit Steven Pinker, who praised Wilson's "excellent" book in 1998 and calls for consilience between science and the humanities in his 2018 bestseller *Enlightenment Now*. The major difference between Wilson and Pinker is stylistic. Whereas Wilson holds out an olive branch to "postmodern" humanities scholars who challenge science's objectivity and authority, Pinker scolds them. Pinker accuses postmodernists of "defiant obscurantism, self-refuting relativism and suffocating political correctness."

The enduring appeal of consilience makes it worth revisiting. Consilience raises two big questions: (1) Is it feasible? (2) Is it desirable? Feasibility first. As Wilson points out, physics has been an especially potent unifier, establishing over the past few centuries that the heavens and earth are made of the same stuff ruled by the same forces. Now physicists seek a single theory that fuses general relativity, which describes gravity, with quantum field theory, which accounts for electromagnetism and the nuclear forces. This is Hawking's theory of everything and Steven Weinberg's "final theory."

Writing in 1998, Wilson clearly expected physicists to find a theory of everything soon, but today they seem farther than ever from that goal. Worse, they still cannot agree on what quantum mechanics means. As science writer Philip Ball points out in his 2018 book *Beyond Weird: Why Everything You Thought You Knew about Quantum Physics Is Different*, there are more interpretations of quantum mechanics now than ever.

The same is true of scientific attempts to bridge the explanatory chasm between matter and mind. In the 1990s, it still seemed possible that researchers would discover how physical processes in the brain and other systems generate consciousness. Since then, mind-body studies have undergone a paradigm explosion, with theorists espousing a bewildering variety of models, involving quantum mechanics, information theory and Bayesian mathematics. Some researchers suggest that consciousness pervades all matter, a view called panpsychism; others insist that the so-called hard problem of consciousness is a pseudoproblem because consciousness is an "illusion."

There are schisms even within Wilson's own field of evolutionary biology. In *Consilience* and elsewhere, Wilson suggests that natural selection promotes traits at the level of tribes and other groups; in this way, evolution might have bequeathed us a propensity for religion, war and other social behaviors. Other prominent Darwinians, notably Richard Dawkins and Robert Trivers, reject group selection, arguing that natural selection operates only at the level of individual organisms and even individual genes.

If scientists cannot achieve consilience even within specific fields, what hope is there for consilience between, say, quantum chromodynamics and queer theory? (Actually, in her fascinating 2007 book *Meeting the Universe Halfway: Quantum Physics and the Entanglement of Matter and Meaning*, physicist-philosopher Karen Barad finds resonances between physics and gender politics; but Barad's book represents the kind of postmodern analysis deplored by Wilson and Pinker.) If consilience entails convergence toward a consensus, science is moving *away* from consilience.

So, consilience doesn't look feasible, at least not at the moment. Next question: Is consilience *desirable*? Although I've always doubted whether it *could* happen, I once thought consilience *should* happen.

If humanity can agree on a single, rational worldview, maybe we can do a better job solving our shared problems, like climate change, inequality, pandemics and militarism. We could also get rid of bad ideas, such as the notion that God likes some of us more than others; or that racial and sexual inequality and war are inevitable consequences of our biology.

I also saw theoretical diversity, or pluralism, as philosophers call it, as a symptom of failure; the abundance of "solutions" to the mind-body problem, like the abundance of treatments for cancer, means that none works very well. But increasingly, I see pluralism as a valuable, even necessary counterweight to our yearning for certitude. Pluralism is especially important when it comes to our ideas about who we are, can be and should be. If we settle on a single self-conception, we risk limiting our freedom to reinvent ourselves, to discover new ways to flourish.

Wilson acknowledges that consilience is a reductionistic enterprise, which will eliminate many ways of seeing the world. Consider how he treats mystical visions, in which we seem to glimpse truths normally hidden behind the surface of things. To my mind, these experiences rub our faces in the unutterable weirdness of existence, which transcends all our knowledge and forms of expression. As William James says in *The Varieties of Religious Experience*, mystical experiences should "forbid a premature closing of our accounts with reality."

Wilson disagrees. He thinks mystical experiences are reducible to physiological processes. In *Consilience*, he focuses on Peruvian shaman-artist Pablo Amaringo, whose paintings depict fantastical, jungly visions induced by ayahuasca, a hallucinogenic tea (which I happen to have taken) brewed from two Amazonian plants. Wilson attributes the snakes that slither through Amaringo's paintings to natural selection, which instilled an adaptive fear of snakes in our ancestors; it should not be surprising that snakes populate many religious myths, such as the biblical story of Eden.

Moreover, ayahuasca contains psychotropic compounds, including the potent psychedelic dimethyltryptamine, like those that induce dreams, which stem from, in Wilson's words, the "editing of information in the memory banks of the brain" that occurs while we sleep. These nightly neural discharges are "arbitrary in content," that is, meaningless; but the brain desperately tries to assemble them into "coherent narratives," which we experience as dreams.

In this way, Wilson "explains" Amaringo's visions in terms of evolutionary biology, psychology and neurochemistry. This is a spectacular example of what Paul Feyerabend, my favorite philosopher and a fierce advocate for pluralism, calls "the tyranny of truth." Wilson imposes his materialistic, secular worldview on the shaman, and he strips ayahuasca visions of any genuine spiritual significance. While he exalts biological diversity, Wilson shows little respect for the diversity of human beliefs.

Wilson is a gracious, courtly man in person as well on the page. But his consilience project stems from excessive faith in science, or scientism. (Both Wilson and Pinker embrace the term *scientism*, and they no doubt think that the phrase "excessive faith in science" is oxymoronic.) Given the failure to achieve consilience within physics and biology—not to mention the replication crisis and other problems—scientists should stop indulging in fantasies about conquering all human culture and attaining something akin to omniscience. Scientists, in short, should be more humble.

Ironically, Wilson himself questioned the desirability of final knowledge early in his career. At the end of his 1975 masterpiece *Sociobiology*, Wilson anticipates the themes of *Consilience*, predicting that evolutionary theory plus genetics will soon absorb the social sciences and humanities. But Wilson doesn't exult at this prospect. When we can explain ourselves in "mechanistic terms," he warns, "the result might be hard to accept"; we might find ourselves, as Camus put it, "divested of illusions."

Wilson needn't have worried. Scientific omniscience looks less likely than ever, and humans are far too diverse, creative and contrary to settle for a single worldview of any kind. Inspired by mysticism and the arts, as well as by science, we will keep arguing about who we are and reinventing ourselves forever. Is consilience a bad idea, which we'd be better off without? I wouldn't go that far. Like utopia, another byproduct of our yearning for perfection, consilience, the dream of total knowledge, can serve as a useful goad to the imagination, as long as we see it as an unreachable ideal. Let's just hope we never think we've reached it.

This is an opinion and analysis article; the views expressed by the author or authors are not necessarily those of Scientific American.

About the Author

John Horgan directs the Center for Science Writings at the Stevens Institute of Technology. His books include The End of Science, The End of War and Mind-Body Problems, *available for free at mindbodyproblems.com. For many years he wrote the popular blog Cross Check for* Scientific American.

Free Will Is Only an Illusion if You Are, Too

By Alessandra Buccella and Tomáš Dominik

Imagine you are shopping online for a new pair of headphones. There is an array of colors, brands and features to look at. You feel that you can pick any model that you like and are in complete control of your decision. When you finally click the "add to shopping cart" button, you believe that you are doing so out of your own free will.

But what if we told you that while you thought that you were still browsing, your brain activity had already highlighted the headphones you would pick? That idea may not be so far-fetched. Though neuroscientists likely could not predict your choice with 100 percent accuracy, research has demonstrated that some information about your upcoming action is present in brain activity several seconds before you even become conscious of your decision.

As early as the 1960s, studies found that when people perform a simple, spontaneous movement, their brain exhibits a buildup in neural activity—what neuroscientists call a "readiness potential"—before they move. In the 1980s, neuroscientist Benjamin Libet reported this readiness potential even preceded a person's reported *intention* to move, not just their movement. In 2008 a group of researchers found that some information about an upcoming decision is present in the brain up to 10 seconds in advance, long before people reported making the decision of when or how to act.

These studies have sparked questions and debates. To many observers, these findings debunked the intuitive concept of free will. After all, if neuroscientists can infer the timing or choice of your movements long before you are consciously aware of your decision, perhaps people are merely puppets, pushed around by neural processes unfolding below the threshold of consciousness.

But as researchers who study volition from both a neuroscientific and philosophical perspective, we believe that there's still much more to this story. We work with a collaboration of philosophers and scientists to provide more nuanced interpretations–including a better understanding of the readiness potential–and a more fruitful theoretical framework in which to place them. The conclusions suggest "free will" remains a useful concept, although people may need to reexamine how they define it.

Let's start from a commonsense observation: much of what people do each day is arbitrary. We put one foot in front of the other when we start walking. Most of the time, we do not actively deliberate about which leg to put forward first. It doesn't matter. The same is true for many other actions and choices. They are largely meaningless and irreflective.

Most empirical studies of free will–including Libet's–have focused on these kinds of arbitrary actions. In such actions, researchers can indeed "read out" our brain activity and trace information about our movements and choices before we even realize we are about to make them. But if these actions don't matter to us, is it all that notable that they are initiated unconsciously? More significant decisions–such as whether to take a job, get married or move to a different country–are infinitely more interesting and complex and are quite consciously made.

If we start working with a more philosophically grounded understanding of free will, we realize that only a small subset of our everyday actions is important enough to worry about. We want to feel in control of those decisions, the ones whose outcomes make a difference in our life and whose responsibility we feel on our shoulders. It is in this context–decisions that *matter*–that the question of free will most naturally applies.

In 2019 neuroscientists Uri Maoz, Liad Mudrik and their colleagues investigated that idea. They presented participants with a choice of two nonprofit organizations to which they could donate $1,000. People could indicate their preferred organization by pressing the left or right button. In some cases, participants knew that their choice mattered because the button would determine which organization would receive the full $1,000. In other cases, people knowingly made meaningless choices because they were told that both organizations would receive $500 regardless of their selection. The results were somewhat surprising. Meaningless choices were preceded by a readiness potential, just as in previous experiments. *Meaningful* choices were not, however. When we care about a decision and its outcome, our brain appears to behave differently than when a decision is arbitrary.

Even more interesting is the fact that ordinary people's intuitions about free will and decision-making do not seem consistent with these findings. Some of our colleagues, including Maoz and neuroscientist Jake Gavenas, recently published the results of a large survey, with more than 600 respondents, in which they asked people to rate how "free" various choices made by others seemed. Their ratings suggested that people do not recognize that the brain may handle meaningful choices in a different way from more arbitrary or meaningless ones. People tend, in other words, to imagine all their choices–from which sock to put on first to where to spend a vacation–as equally "free," even though neuroscience suggests otherwise.

What this tells us is that free will may exist, but it may not operate in the way we intuitively imagine. In the same vein, there is a second intuition that must be addressed to understand studies of volition. When experiments have found that brain activity, such as the readiness potential, precedes the conscious intention to act, some people have jumped to the conclusion that they are "not in charge." They do not have free will, they reason, because they are somehow subject to their brain activity.

But that assumption misses a broader lesson from neuroscience. "We" are our brain. The combined research makes clear that human beings do have the power to make conscious choices. But that agency and accompanying sense of personal responsibility are not supernatural. They happen in the brain, regardless of whether scientists observe them as clearly as they do a readiness potential.

So there is no "ghost" inside the cerebral machine. But as researchers, we argue that this machinery is so complex, inscrutable and mysterious that popular concepts of "free will" or the "self" remain incredibly useful. They help us think through and imagine—albeit imperfectly—the workings of the mind and brain. As such, they can guide and inspire our investigations in profound ways—provided we continue to question and test these assumptions along the way.

About the Authors

Alessandra Buccella is a philosopher at the Institute for Interdisciplinary Brain and Behavioral Sciences at Chapman University. She studies the theoretical foundations of cognitive neuroscience, psychology and artificial intelligence.

Tomáš Dominik is an experimental psychologist at the Institute for Interdisciplinary Brain and Behavioral Sciences at Chapman University. He studies physiological and neural correlates of consciousness and volition. In his research, Dominik replicated neuroscientist Benjamin Libet's 1980s experiment on brain activity and people's reported intention, or urge, to move but also showed a problem with Libet's method of "measuring" this intention.

Where's My Consciousness-ometer?

By Tam Hunt

How do you know your dog is conscious? Well, she wags her tail when she's happy, bounces around like a young human child when excited, and yawns when sleepy–among many other examples of behaviors that convince us (most of us, at least) that dogs are quite conscious in ways that are similar to, but not the same as, human consciousness.

Most of us are okay attributing emotions, desires, pain and pleasure–which is what I mean by consciousness in this context–to dogs and many other pets.

What about further down the chain. Is a mouse conscious? We can apply similar tests for "behavioral correlates of consciousness" like those I've just mentioned, but, for some of us, the mice behaviors observed will be considerably less convincing than for dogs in terms of there being an inner life for the average mouse.

What about an ant? What behaviors do ants engage in that might make us think an individual ant is at least a little bit conscious? Or is it not conscious at all?

Let me now turn the questions around: how do I know you, my dear reader, are conscious? If we met, I'd probably introduce myself and hear you say your name and respond to my questions and various small talk. You might be happy to meet me and smile or shake my hand vigorously. Or you might get a little anxious at meeting someone new and behave awkwardly. All of these behaviors would convince me that you are in fact conscious much like I am, and not just faking it!

Now here's the broader question? How can we know anybody or any animal or any thing is *actually* conscious and not just faking it? The nature of consciousness makes it by necessity a wholly private affair. The only consciousness I can know with *certainty* is my own. Everything else is inference.

So, where's my consciousness-ometer?

These questions are more than philosophical. With the coming age of intelligent digital assistants, self-driving cars and other robots serving us and increasingly running our lives, does it matter if these AIs are actually conscious or just faking it?

Perhaps more relevant today, how can we know that coma victims, or patients in vegetative or minimally conscious states, are conscious or not?

This is an active area of research and for the poor victims in these categories, plus their families and loved ones, these questions are deadly serious. How can a family know whether to take a patient off life support or not, if they don't know with any certainty what kind of consciousness is or is not present?

In my work, often with psychologist Jonathan Schooler at the University of California, Santa Barbara, we're developing a framework for thinking about the many different ways to possibly test for the presence of consciousness—all using, necessarily, a process of reasonable inference.

There is a small but growing field looking at how to assess the presence and even quantity of consciousness in various entities. I've divided possible tests into three broad categories that I call the measurable correlates of consciousness, or MCC.

Neural Correlates of Consciousness and "Signatures of Consciousness"

When determining whether a vegetative patient is conscious in any way, we can and do examine the neural correlates of consciousness only, since there aren't any behaviors to observe and no creative products either. Various researchers have proposed tests for cognition and consciousness in coma and vegetative patients.

What's physically going on in the brain? Neuroimaging tools such as EEG, MEG, fMRI and transcranial magnetic stimulation (each with their own strengths and weaknesses), are able to provide information on activity happening within the brain even in coma and vegetative patients.

Stanislas Dehaene, a French neuroscientist, has identified four "signatures of consciousness," which extend the idea of neural correlates of consciousness to more specific aspects of brain activity that are necessary for conscious awareness. He focuses on what's known as the "P3 wave" in the dorsolateral cortex as the single most important signature of consciousness in humans. And in tests of vegetative and minimally conscious patients, he and his colleagues have successfully predicted which patients are most likely to regain more normal states of consciousness.

Sid Kouider, another French neuroscientist, has examined very young babies in order to assess the likelihood of them being conscious. He concludes (unsurprisingly) that even newborns are conscious in various complex ways.

Behavioral Correlates of Consciousness

When we are considering potential conscious entities that can't communicate directly, and that won't let us put our neuroscientific measurement tools on their head (if they even have heads), we need to consider behavioral correlates as clues for the presence and type of consciousness.

For example, are cats conscious? The brain architecture in cats is quite different from humans, and they have very minimal prefrontal cortex, which is thought to be the center of many higher-order activities of the human brain. But is prefrontal cortex necessary for consciousness?

Cat behavior is complex and pretty easy to map onto human behavior in many ways. The fact that cats purr, flex their toes and snuggle when petted, in similar ways to humans demonstrating pleasure when physically stimulated (minus the purrs, of course), meow loudly for food when hungry, and stop meowing when fed, demonstrate curiosity or fear about other cats or humans with various types of body language, and many other behaviors that we can easily observe ourselves if we have cats as pets, is all pretty convincing evidence, for most of us, that cats are indeed conscious and have a rich emotional life.

Creative Correlates of Consciousness

Creative output is another source of information for assessing the presence of consciousness. If for whatever reason we can't examine neural or behavioral correlates of consciousness, we may be able to examine the creative products of consciousness for clues.

For example, when we examine ancient architectural structures such as Stonehenge or cave paintings in Europe that have been judged to be as much as 65,000 years old, are we reasonable in judging the creators of these items to be conscious in ways similar to our own? Most of us would say: obviously, yes. We know from experience that it would take high intelligence and consciousness to produce such items today, so we reasonably conclude that our ancient ancestors had similar levels of consciousness.

What if we find obviously unnatural artifacts on Mars or other bodies in our solar system? Do we reasonably infer that whatever entities created such artifacts were conscious? It will depend on the artifacts in question, but if we were to find anything remotely similar to human dwellings or machinery on other planets, but which was clearly not human in origin, most of us would reasonably infer that the creators of these artifacts were also conscious.

Closer to home, artificial intelligence (AI) has produced some pretty impressive art, fetching over $400,000 at a recent art auction. At what point do reasonable people conclude that amazing art creation requires consciousness? We can conduct a kind of "artistic Turing test" and ask study participants to consider various works of art and say which ones they conclude must have been created by a human. And if AI artwork consistently fools people into thinking it was made by a human, is that good evidence to conclude that the AI is at least in some ways conscious?

There is not yet a "consciousness-ometer," but various researchers have suggested ideas, including Dehaene, and Italian-American researcher Giulio Tononi and his colleagues, who focus on "integrated information" as a measure of consciousness.

Neuroscientist Giulio Tononi and his colleagues like Christof Koch focus on what they call "integrated information" as a measure of consciousness. This theory suggests that anything that integrates at least one bit of information has at least a tiny amount of consciousness. A light diode, for example, contains just one bit of information and thus has a very limited type of consciousness. With just two possible states, on or off, however, it's a rather uninteresting kind of consciousness.

In my work, my collaborators and I share this "panpsychist" foundation. We accept as a working hypothesis that any physical system has some associated consciousness, however small it may be in the vast majority of cases.

Rather than integrated information as the key measure of consciousness, however, we focus on resonance and synchronization and the degree to which parts of a whole resonate at the same or similar frequencies. Resonance in the case of the human brain generally means shared electric field oscillation rates, such as gamma band synchrony (40–120 hertz) as one example.

Our consciousness-ometer would, insofar as it focuses on neural correlates of consciousness, look at the degree of shared resonance of various types, and resulting information flows, as the measure of consciousness. Humans and other mammals enjoy a particularly rich kind of consciousness, because there are many levels of pervasive shared synchronization throughout the brain, nervous system and body.

In our framework more generally, we propose a "weight of the evidence" approach to assessing the presence and nature of consciousness in any particular object of study. We ask a number of questions, in all areas of MCC as described above, to the object of study, and it answers in whatever ways it can. We then make the same kinds of reasonable inferences about the presence and nature of consciousness that we do every day when it comes to other humans or animals. This questioning process is meant to be truly general and could apply to any object of study.

The logical chain of this framework is straightforward: I know I'm conscious; I assume you are conscious because you act a lot like me and do many smart things; I engage in similar reasonable inferences when assessing whether various animals are conscious and to what degree; we can use the same process of reasonable inference all the way down the chain of physical complexity.

Tests for consciousness are still in their infancy. But this field of study is undergoing a renaissance because the study of consciousness more generally has finally become a respectable scientific pursuit. Before too long it may be possible to measure just how much consciousness is present in various entities–including in you and me.

The views expressed are those of the author(s) and are not necessarily those of Scientific American.

About the Author

Tam Hunt is a scholar and writer, with a focus on the philosophy of mind, and is affiliated with the University of California, Santa Barbara. He is author of Eco, Ego, Eros: Essays in Philosophy, Spirituality, and Science *and blogs at Medium.com.*

GLOSSARY

anesthesia A drug or medication that causes temporary insensitivity to pain and in some cases a loss of awareness.

causal When one event, state, or object results in the production of another and is at least partly the cause of it.

coma A prolonged, deep state of unconsciousness and unresponsiveness.

consciousness One's experience and awareness of internal and external existence.

consilience Agreement between different academic disciplines in how they approach a topic, especially the sciences and humanities.

correlate Two things that are connected and affect one another. If something happens to one variable, there will also be a change in the other.

intrinsic A quality that is essential to something's nature; in philosophy it is also something that is valuable on its own.

neologorrheic Characterized by making up new words, known as neologisms.

panpsychism The theory that consciousness is a fundamental and ubiquitous characteristic of the universe and all matter within it.

psilocybin A naturally occurring psychedelic compound found in various species of fungi, sometimes known as "magic mushrooms."

qualia The way external sensory experiences and perceptions are experienced internally and subjectively.

FURTHER INFORMATION

Fins, Jason J. "Neuroethics and Disorders of Consciousness: Discerning Brain States in Clinical Practice and Research," *AMA Journal of Ethics*, December 2016. https://journalofethics.ama-assn.org/article/neuroethics-and-disorders-consciousness-discerning-brain-states-clinical-practice-and-research/2016-12.

Goff, Philip. "Science as We Know It Can't Explain Consciousness—but a Revolution Is Coming," The Conversation, November 1, 2019. https://theconversation.com/science-as-we-know-it-cant-explain-consciousness-but-a-revolution-is-coming-126143.

Herwig, Uwe. "Me, Myself, and I: How the Brain Maintains a Sense of Self," *Scientific American*, July 1, 2010. https://www.scientificamerican.com/article/me-myself-and-i/.

Koch, Christof. "This Is Your Brain on Drugs," *Scientific American*, May 1, 2012. https://www.scientificamerican.com/article/this-is-your-brain-on-drugs/.

MacCormack, Patricia. "Animal Consciousness: Why It's Time to Rethink Our Human-Centred Approach," The Conversation, April 18, 2023. https://theconversation.com/animal-consciousness-why-its-time-to-rethink-our-human-centred-approach-201533.

Schurger, Aaron, and Michael Graziano. "Consciousness Explained or Described?" *Neuroscience of Consciousness*, January 1, 2022. https://academic.oup.com/nc/article/2022/1/niac001/6523097.

Zarate, Jean Mary, and Anil Seth. "Marvelling at the Mystery of Consciousness Through a Scientific Lens," *Nature*, February 24, 2023. https://www.nature.com/articles/d41586-023-00545-9.

CITATIONS

1.1 What Is Consciousness? by Christof Koch (June 1, 2018); 1.2 Self-Awareness with a Simple Brain by Ferris Jabr (November 1, 2012); 1.3 Is Consciousness Real? by John Horgan (March 21, 2017); 1.4 Think of Consciousness as Art Created by the Brain by Nicholas Humphrey (May 1, 2015); 1.5 Constant Shifts between Mental States Mark a Signature of Consciousness by Simon Makin (March 12, 2020); 2.1 Transcending the Brain by Bernardo Kastrup (March 29, 2017); 2.2 Me, Myself and My Stranger: Understanding the Neuroscience of Selfhood by Ferris Jabr (September 21, 2010); 2.3 Could Multiple Personality Disorder Explain Life, the Universe and Everything? by Bernardo Kastrup, Adam Crabtree, Edward F. Kelly (June 18, 2018); 2.4 The Science of Altering Consciousness by Gareth Cook (May 15, 2018); 2.5 What Psychedelic Research Can and Cannot Tell Us about Consciousness by Anil Seth, Michael Schartner, Enzo Tagliazucchi, Suresh Muthukumaraswamy, Robin Carhart-Harris, Adam Barrett (October 26, 2018); 2.6 How Can We Tell If a Comatose Patient Is Conscious? by Anouk Bercht, Steven Laureys (August 23, 2018); 2.7 What Doctors Don't Understand about Anesthesia by Stephen Dougherty (February 28, 2012); 3.1 Are Humans the Only Conscious Animal? by Susan Blackmore (September 1, 2018); 3.2 Do Fish Suffer? by John Horgan (November 21, 2017); 3.3 Does Consciousness Pervade the Universe? by Gareth Cook (January 14, 2020); 3.4 Is Anyone Home? A Way to Find Out If AI Has Become Self-Aware by Susan Schneider and Edwin Turner (July 19, 2017); 3.5 We Shouldn't Try to Make Conscious Software—Until We Should by Jim Davies (May 18, 2022); 3.6 Google Engineer Claims AI Chatbot Is Sentient: Why That Matters by Leonardo De Cosmo (July 12, 2022); 3.7 Jellyfish, Sexbots and the Solipsism Problem by John Horgan (December 4, 2017); 4.1 New Technique Seeks to Measure Consciousness by Christof Koch (March 1, 2013); 4.2 Will Science Ever Solve the Mysteries of Consciousness, Free Will and God? by Michael Shermer (July 1, 2018); 4.3 Computers Determine States of Consciousness by Sam Rose (December 18, 2018); 4.4 What God, Quantum Mechanics and Consciousness Have in Common by John Horgan (August 14, 2021); 4.5 *On Consciousness: Science and Subjectivity:* A Q&A with Bernard Baars by Scott Barry Kaufman (May 26, 2020); 4.6 Science Should Not Try to Absorb Religion and Other Ways of Knowing by John Horgan (June 25, 2021); 4.7 Free Will Is Only an Illusion if You Are, Too by Alessandra Buccella, Tomáš Dominik (January 16, 2023); 4.8 Where's My Consciousness-ometer? by Tam Hunt (August 30, 2019)

Each author biography was accurate at the time the article was originally published.

INDEX